The LLC Beginner's Guide

*An Easy and Up-to-Date Guide on How to
Form, Manage, and Scale a Profitable
Limited Liability Company*

Richard Hedberg

Your Free Gift

As a way of saying thank you for your purchase, I'm offering the ebook, *Marketing on Click LLC: A Business Plan Example*, for FREE to my readers.

To get instant access, just go to:
https://ll-publishing.aweb.page/LLC-free-bonus

Inside this ebook you will discover:

• Insider knowledge on formatting and structuring a winning business plan
• Proven strategies for what information to include and how to present it
• Secrets to using the right language and terminology to capture the attention of investors
• Exclusive insights on identifying potential gaps or weaknesses in your own plan
• The key to creating a business proposal that sets you apart from the competition
• And so much more!

Don't miss out on this opportunity to unlock the secrets of a winning business plan. Grab your free ebook today and start creating a plan that will take your business to the next level!

Introduction

Chase the vision, not the money; the money will end up following you.
–Tony Hsieh

I love running businesses, but I struggled in the beginning with one common enemy that disrupted my mindset when it came to starting and managing one. I guess it is probably pretty obvious from the theme and title of the book—I was intimidated by the laws and all the legal terms and conditions involved. It was only after the initial excitement surrounding business ownership had faded a little that I began to really feel the pressure as I started to spend more time and effort educating myself about the process. Nevertheless, you can't escape these aspects as an entrepreneur in modern society, and the laws and regulations will need to be considered with every step you take.

So what happened between then and now that helped me through this initial trepidation? My journey to understanding and actually enjoying the legal side of things couldn't be more hilarious. One day, I started reading a few corporate law books to try to understand all the benefits that come from picking the right legal structure for a business. If you are hearing about this for the first time, a business's legal structure, or business entity, is basically how your business is legally classified under the law. Each has certain regulations with which your business must comply. In a nutshell, it is the legal structure classification that defines your business's liability, tax filing, and other administrative aspects.

I experienced the importance of choosing the right legal structure with one of my very first businesses—a trucking startup. Now, at this time, the trucking business was new to me. Even though I had a pretty robust business plan to assist me, it was still an unfamiliar industry. Over time, however, I began to understand how the business worked, and I soon became successful while meeting multiple business goals with my trucking company. I even wrote a book about it in which I shared my knowledge on how to succeed in the trucking business.

This wasn't a smooth process, however, and amidst all that, there was a time when things weren't going too well. In fact, I was completely stressed out about the fact that this startup could really damage my life. What happens if my personal finances get mixed up with my business? What if I get sued by an unhappy customer? Moreover, I wasn't really getting many clients at the time. I wanted so badly for the business to grow and expand, but it was clearly not happening for me. In a funny way, the business legal structure—something that I wasn't interested in initially—was the answer all along. With the right information, I would boost my business's success and also earn some peace of mind.

Three Magical Letters That Changed Everything

The best way to explain this is to see yourself as an entrepreneur. Imagine your life as a piece of land, and as an entrepreneur, your land is going to be divided into two major areas—one portion is your business life, and the other portion is your personal life. Now, this curiosity about how these portions work together is common to most entrepreneurs, and it definitely kept me up at night. Even though the trucking industry was lucrative, it did come with some risks on a day-to-day basis. What if I mix up my personal assets, finances, and credit with the business part of my life? Or what if one day, one of my trucks hurts someone? What if I get sued and I lose my personal assets?

This is the beauty of having a legal structure, especially an LLC. When your business registers for an LLC, you are basically building a gigantic wall—think the Great Wall of China—between your personal and business portions of land in our allegory. This wall can be called the corporate veil, and the purpose of this wall is to protect entrepreneurs from legal and tax risks when it comes to their businesses. It ensures that your business land won't interfere or mix with your personal land. Almost immediately after filing the paperwork and registering my trucking company as an LLC, I began to sleep easy once again.

The instant benefits I received from doing this were evident. My personal assets were protected. That meant my house and car would never be involved in any legal proceedings if there was a situation where my business got into legal trouble. The next benefit had to do with the tax incentives. Being registered as an LLC helped my business to be more tax efficient. It also removed the extra paperwork involved, as the administrative side of things was much more simple than when I had no legal structure classification in place.

Lastly, registering for an LLC instantly made my trucking company look more professional in the eyes of the market. More clients started taking interest, the calls started pouring in, I received more positive feedback, and I landed more contracts—all because of those three golden letters. It is still amazing when I think about it to this day. The fact that my business was now an LLC simply gave my trucking company a professional image, and this was the appeal that I had been lacking before. People just tend to trust a business more when they see that they're an established entity with a legal structure printed alongside the name.

This Book Will Convince You to Register for an LLC

Now that I've shared my story, I'm sure you are excited and ready to learn all about registering your own business as an LLC. It can change your life. But this isn't the only reason I wrote this book for you. I believe all success starts with the initiative to take action and start learning. Without this step, you will never wrap your mind around the importance of education as an entrepreneur.

You've come this far with the initiative to pick up this book, so I believe you share the same excitement I felt when I first began. I know that anything related to law can be a complex and intimidating subject, and you may even feel the temptation to put those things off until later. I don't blame you, because I've been there, and that leads me to the main reason I created this guide.

Introduction

This book is designed to break that barrier and fill you in on the details by providing useful lessons related to a Limited Liability Company as well as offering a step-by-step guide to forming and managing your own LLC business.

With the beginner in mind, this book uses simple language that gets straight to the point so you can fully absorb the information you need to understand all about LLCs and how to compare them with other business legal structures.

I hope to convince you that no matter how many businesses you go on to start, this legal structure can streamline your path to success just like it did for me. I wish you an enjoyable read, and don't worry—learning about law isn't so bad after all, and you might even enjoy learning all about it from this book. Let's get started!

Chapter 1

The Basics of LLCs

The limited liability corporation is the greatest single invention of modern times.

— Nicholas Murray Butler

We will start our first chapter by providing you with a pure theoretical lesson on the basics of LLCs. I won't bore you with more information than you need, and I'll get straight to the point using simple language, as promised.

By the time you finish reading this chapter, you will have learned an accurate definition of an LLC, its importance, the types of businesses that are ideal for forming an LLC, and the legal requirements and considerations required.

Let's dive straight in.

Understanding the LLC: An Overview

Let's start with defining what an LLC is. In simple terms, an LLC is basically a legal entity that is separate from its owners, thus enabling the entity to have its own assets, enter into independent contractual agreements, and conduct business as its own entity rather than in the owner's name. This was illustrated by the analogy we used in the introduction of having a corporate veil or legal wall in place to separate your business life from your personal life, thus removing any worries of legal risk and allowing you to sleep well every night. By registering the articles of organization (which will be explained later in the chapter) with a state agency, LLCs are formed under state law, and in an LLC, members can be individuals, corporations, or other entities.

But you may be wondering, how are LLCs any different from other business structures? For starters, in an LLC, members or shareholders are not personally liable for the business's obligations, such as debts, and this acts as a safeguard to protect the owners' personal assets. Secondly, when it comes to taxes, you will see that LLCs are not taxed as an entity. For example, your business's profits (or losses) are passed through to the members' tax returns—yes!—individually.

To understand this better, imagine that you own a majority of shares in your LLC company; the profit made by your company doesn't get taxed at a business level but is instead passed through, depending on the majority of shares you own, and it will only be taxed as your personal income. This means the profits or losses don't go through double taxation. And lastly, there are fewer formalities involved in LLCs when compared to corporations, for instance. You will have fewer requirements when it comes to administrative tasks, and members will have the freedom to manage operations by themselves.

So, to sum it all up, an LLC is unique when compared to other business structures because:

- it protects the members' personal assets, unlike sole proprietorships and partnerships.
- it is easy to form, with minimal cost and paperwork involved.
- owners or members have flexibility when it comes to adding more shareholders and also managing day-to-day operations.
- members' profits don't go through double taxation, unlike corporations.
- as I mentioned earlier at the start of this book, these three magical letters automatically transform your business and make it more credible and professional.

In the next chapter, you will learn more about the other business structures and how LLCs come out on top when compared to them.

Understanding the Cons of Forming an LLC

Even though there are many benefits to be gained by forming an LLC, I would like to keep this book transparent and inform you about the downsides that should be considered as part of your due diligence when starting a business. There are always both advantages and disadvantages when it comes to making big moves such as this one, but this is also why I enjoy being an entrepreneur. What matters most is that you assess whether the pros outweigh the cons, and this will all depend on how you look at it.

One of the biggest disadvantages of forming an LLC—you might know exactly where I'm going with this—is the self-employment tax. Despite the fact that LLCs boast the pass-through taxation benefit when compared to other business structures, self-employment taxes here are generally higher when compared to income taxes for normal employees. You may even find the calculation of self-employment taxes for an LLC to be quite complex when compared to the traditional income tax. So, that's one major con. Another thing to consider when managing an LLC is its lifespan. For example, suppose a member or owner either leaves or passes away; what are the repercussions regarding continuation in the oper-ating agreement? This can depend on the rules and regula-tions in place for each state.

And oh boy, speaking of state regulations... These are another potential negative you should keep in mind if you choose to register your business, as each state's laws will entail varying costs and administrative requirements—and that could lead to more paperwork, such as filing annual reports and ensuring proper documentation is maintained at all times.

Lastly, another consideration before forming an LLC is your options for raising capital. This is because, when compared to other entities such as corporations, you will find that LLCs run into unique challenges along the way when it comes to raising capital through the sale of stock, mainly because they cannot match the shares that a corporation has.

However, as I mentioned earlier, it is all about whether the pros outweigh the cons for your situation, but I have found that, with some strategic decisions such as hiring the right accountants, implementing the right administrative procedures in your organization, and planning ahead financially, you can mitigate these disadvantages quite easily.

What It Takes to Establish an LLC

Now, let us get into the legal requirements for establishing an LLC. You will find that these will vary slightly across different states in the U.S. Nevertheless, I've narrowed it down to the most common things you need to have in mind and on your checklist to ensure you have formed an LLC properly.

So, prepare a checklist and note down the following:

1. Choose a business name during the registration process.
2. Have a registered agent on hand.
3. Prepare and file the articles of organization.
4. Draft an operating agreement.
5. Get permits and licenses.
6. Apply for an Employer Identification Number (EIN).
7. Meet compliance requirements for your state.
8. Open a business bank account.
9. Register for state and local taxes.

All of these will be discussed in-depth in Chapter 3 (Forming an LLC), and you will soon understand the actions you need to take in order to tick these off your checklist.

Types of Businesses That Utilize the LLC Model

I don't want to keep raving about how versatile and robust LLCs are. It's better that you see it for yourself, especially since I am going to tell you about the types of businesses that utilize the LLC structure and are ideal for it. This will give you a real-life idea of how significant forming an LLC can be.

Small Businesses and Startups

For starters, forming an LLC is a popular choice among many small businesses—that includes startups and local businesses like restaurants, cafés, consulting firms, etc.—because it's simple to create. You will find that many family-owned businesses have LLCs in their name because it can help protect their family members from personal liability, as well as help them gain flexibility with ownership and management.

Professional Services

Even professional services, including lawyers, accountants, doctors, and other consultants, use LLCs in order to protect their personal assets, benefit from pass-through taxation, and add a touch of credibility to their business name. The list doesn't stop there, as most creative agencies such as digital marketing providers and design and photography studios make use of LLCs as well.

Modern-Day Businesses

Many retail businesses, which include both online stores and brick-and-mortar businesses, utilize the LLC structure. Another good example to look at is tech startups in your country. Most end up choosing the LLC structure because it guarantees ease of operation, and this provides the upper management with more freedom to focus on their core-business aspects, such as product development and investing in research and development (R&D).

Real Estate Investments

When looking at other industries, you will find that real estate ventures, such as rental property businesses, use LLCs. The real estate market can be a high-risk industry, so this structure acts as a shield to protect these companies from potential lawsuits and having their personal assets seized as a result.

Joint Ventures

Even joint ventures (when two or more businesses form a shared ownership) utilize the LLC, since it provides flexible ownership and management structures.

As you can see, the LLC is a truly versatile model that most businesses lean into. It can be beneficial to have it as part of your own business structure in the long run.

Keep These in Mind Before Forming an LLC

Before concluding this chapter, it is essential for you to know that forming an LLC does require a few careful considerations, and as a determined entrepreneur, you must keep certain aspects in mind at all times. The common considerations you need to have include the following:

Have a business plan.

A business plan simply helps you to outline all your business goals and understand your target audience, your key product and services, financial projections, and the marketing strategies to deliver your unique value proposition. This step is very important to me, and I believe it can make or break your success.

Do the research in advance.

It is vital to do some research early, especially when it comes to the legal and financial implications. This might include understanding the costs involved in the registration process, knowing the taxes you need to register for, state laws, compliance requirements, and other licensing requirements involved in your particular industry. Keep in mind, especially if you are based in the U.S., that each state has its own set of regulations, and that means registration fees will vary along with other legal obligations. Do the research in advance and assemble your resources accordingly.

Refresh yourself on tax regulations.

Understanding the tax implications involved before forming an LLC is crucial. You know it provides pass-through taxation; however, it is best to have a much deeper understanding. Consider consulting with a tax professional to learn the types of taxes involved and how this can affect your personal tax filing. Make sure you're taking care of taxes correctly to avoid breaking the law inadvertently, as this can have serious repercussions.

Is the name available?

You will be disappointed if you've thought up a name that you're excited about only to find it is unavailable when you look it up in your state's business naming database. I have a friend who was despondent when he couldn't get his preferred business name and had to think of something else that wasn't nearly as catchy. His business is doing okay, but he secretly still hates his business's name, I can tell. Therefore, check with your state's database early on and be sure to have a few good choices picked out to fall back on. You'll want to have this established before considering other registration-based requirements, such as appointing a registered agent who will receive your official and legal documents on behalf of the business.

Don't forget about your legal requirements checklist.

It is important for you to remember that you have a checklist of things to tick off. Some tasks can be easy to overlook, like obtaining your permits and licenses, drafting an operating agreement, opening a business bank account, and applying for an EIN.

An LLC doesn't protect you from personal misconduct.

It is important to keep in mind that even though LLCs protect your personal assets from business debts and liabilities, it doesn't necessarily mean that you are fully protected. If there is personal misconduct on your part, this means you can be held liable. Remember that there is a line between your personal and business affairs, and you should never cross that line.

Determine the ownership and management structure.

It would be ideal for you to plan in advance regarding the number of members in your LLC and their particular roles. This also includes deciding whether your LLC will be managed by each member or if there will be a manager appointed to manage the ownership. This can be important before forming an LLC to ensure transparency in ownership and management proceedings.

Seek professional help to guide you.

It is important to have professional advice in your ear at all times, so planning ahead and hiring the right professionals before forming an LLC is key. For example, seek out the best attorneys and accountants in your city and work with them. They can be your guiding light in ensuring your LLC is compliant with all requirements, and also that you don't fall through any loopholes in the system when it comes to personal liability.

Where's your funding capital?

You might have a pretty good idea once you've constructed a solid business plan, but in any case, it's important to know how much capital you're going to need to start your LLC as early as possible. Moreover, you'll need a plan for acquiring this startup capital if you are not funding the whole thing yourself. Some common sources include savings accounts, applying for loans from banks, and attracting startup or angel investors.

What's your long-term vision?

Before starting any business, let alone forming an LLC, you need to consider your long-term vision and goals for your business. You need to first figure out if the LLC structure will encourage growth and progress in your organization, as well as whether it will lead to positive scaling in the long run. Starting a business right means not limiting your perspective to the short-term and the present. You need to think long-term and always look forward to growing through expansion.

What's your exit strategy?

I left this consideration for last, but it is worth keeping in mind. Planning an exit strategy means you have a plan for what you need to do in the case that your business dissolves in the future or you decide to sell it. It is important to know the steps you'll take to wind down your LLC efficiently and ensure your assets are protected. You will learn more about exiting your LLC in Chapter 11.

Key Takeaways From This Chapter

- An LLC is a legal entity that is separate from its owners, thus enabling the entity to have its own assets, enter into contractual agreements, and conduct business as an entity rather than in the owner's name. Remember the analogy of having a big wall separating your personal life and your business life.
- LLCs provide a lot of benefits, such as pass-through taxation, protecting owners' personal assets, fewer formalities, and flexibility in ownership and management structure.
- LLCs do have downsides, and these include self-employment taxes, a limited lifespan, varying state regulations, and a lack of capital-raising options. However, these things can be mitigated with strategic thinking.
- You will need the following things to establish an LLC: business name, registered agent, articles of organization, operating agreement, permits, licenses, EIN, business bank account, registration for state/local taxes, and state compliance requirements.
- Types of businesses suitable for LLCs include small businesses, startups, professional services, family-owned businesses, retail, real estate investments, and joint ventures.

- There are a few considerations you need to keep in mind before forming an LLC, and these include: doing your research, having a solid business plan, understanding the potential risks, seeking professional help, and knowing the implications of having your business converted to an LLC.

Chapter 2

Choosing the Right Structure for Your LLC

In a world that's changing really quickly, the only strategy that is guaranteed to fail is not taking risks.

— Mark Zuckerberg

In this chapter, we will dive deep into choosing the right structure for your LLC, as this decision can depend on a few factors. This chapter will educate you on the significance of opting for an LLC by comparing it first to other business structures such as sole proprietorships, partnerships, corporations, and other business entities.

Additionally, you will come to understand the factors to consider regarding tax implications when comparing single-member LLCs and multi-member LLCs.

Sole Proprietorship or LLC?

Right off the bat, let us first compare the LLC to the sole proprietorship. You can differentiate these two based on the following areas:

Legal structure definition

A sole proprietorship, in legal terms, does not have a distinct legal wall between the business and the owner. So, just imagine the opposite of an LLC in this case. The owner will be personally held liable for any business debts and other legal obligations incurred during his tenure as a sole proprietor. This was something I had to worry about when I was solely running my trucking startup, as I did worry about the legal implications and financial pickle I could get into if my personal assets, such as my house, car, etc., were to be held. In a nutshell, sole proprietorship doesn't offer liability protection. In contrast, LLCs provide that liability protection to you and your shareholders, hence having that wall in between your personal and business assets as protection. However, as mentioned in the previous chapter, this does not guarantee that you will be protected in the case of personal wrongdoings.

Tax implications

In a sole proprietorship, you will find that the owner fills out individual tax returns using Form 1040. This includes paying self-employment taxes on the net income, as well as Social Security and Medicare taxes. If you compare this with LLCs, it is not much different. There is no federal taxation involved, and owners are also being taxed individually. The only difference comes into play with the type of LLC. For example, sole proprietors and single-member LLCs (those which include only you as the shareholder) will pay the same individual taxes based on the business's net profit. Whereas multi-member LLCs (having more than one member) will pay taxes on the business's net profit based on the shares they hold in the company. Hence, you will find some members in a multi-member LLC paying more taxes on a bigger portion of that net profit because they hold a majority of the shares in the company when compared to other members.

Business expansion and growth considerations

In a sole proprietorship, making careful considerations for business expansion and future growth can be an uphill task because sole proprietors have to rely on their own assets, resources, and capital. This can act as a limitation on their business to meet or exceed growth expectations. On the other hand, LLCs often involve multiple members that pool their capital, resources, and even game-changing ideas in order to see massive growth. Moreover, because of the corporate veil protecting their personal assets, this allows shareholders to think freely and take big business actions without feeling that they are taking big personal risks.

Personal risk tolerance and asset protection evaluation

In a sole proprietorship, you will find the owner bearing the brunt of the risk in their business. So, when you evaluate the personal risk involved in a sole proprietorship, it undoubtedly poses a great risk to your personal assets. On the other hand, for LLCs, you already know that there are lower risks involved and that your personal assets are protected from any business debts, obligations, lawsuits, etc.

In a nutshell, the pros of LLCs outweigh the cons of sole proprietorship by a landslide. This is the reason why I moved away from the whole one-man-versus-the-world mindset and eventually opted in for an LLC.

Corporation or LLC?

Now let us compare LLCs with corporations. A corporation is similar to an LLC, but the major difference is that corporations are owned by a group of shareholders, whereas LLCs are owned by one or a few individuals. To make it simple, if you think about corporations, think publicly traded companies, whereas LLCs are basically private companies.

But to truly remove any confusion around the LLC and a corporation, we will compare them based on the following areas:

Simplicity vs. formalities

A big difference between corporations and LLCs lies in one's simplicity versus the other's formalities. For instance, corporations—especially C corps—entail a lot of formalities and administrative-related requirements. For example, there are usually more regular shareholder meetings, more corporate records to be maintained, and more overall compliance to pay attention to regarding corporate governance regulations. On the other hand, we know that LLCs are hailed for their simplicity when it comes to formation and flexibility. Compared to corporations, you will find less paperwork involved, and the operating agreements will provide a detailed overview of the ownership structure, management style, and decision-making process.

Ownership structure, management, and decision-making

In a corporation, you will find that the ownership structure (with its shareholders) is more firm and inflexible. In a nutshell, the board of directors in a corporation is mainly responsible for making strategic decisions and delegating tasks to the management team for daily operations. In contrast, LLCs have a more flexible ownership structure, since members will have varying ownership rights. And this translates to the management structure, too. The operating agreement—which you will learn about in detail in the coming chapters—will outline the managers responsible for handling day-to-day operations.

Tax differences

When looking at taxation implications, this is best explained by how each of these entities' taxation procedure works. For instance, regarding corporations, there are C corps and S corps, and taxation for both of these is surprisingly different. For example, C corporations are subjected to double taxation. That means the corporation is taxed at a corporate tax rate, and then the shareholders involved will be taxed again on their personal tax returns based on the dividends they received. On the other hand, S corporations are similar to LLCs in that they also entail a pass-through taxation procedure. You will find the profit is not taxed at a corporate level but only passed to shareholders and taxed based on their personal tax returns.

Fundraising, venture capital, and IPO potential

When talking about these factors, corporations have varying conditions for C corps and S corps. For instance, S corporations can be limited in their fundraising and venture capital investments capability because there are restrictions on the number and type of shareholders they can claim. On the other hand, C corporations are more suited for fundraising and acquiring venture capital. This is mainly because they issue different stock classes, making it easy to offer equity to investors. This is why C corporations can comfortably go public through an IPO after meeting the required conditions. Now, if you look at LLCs, we have already learned in the section on disadvantages that there can be challenges for LLCs when it comes to raising funds and winning venture capital investments. Moreover, you will find that most angel investors, venture capitalists, etc., choose to invest in corporations more often when compared to LLCs. So, this is probably the biggest con when you compare LLCs to corporations.

Nevertheless, LLCs are still considered the better option compared to corporations mainly because of their simple and flexible nature. Moreover, pass-through taxation and liability protection helps LLCs to expand their business horizons in the long run.

Comparing the LLC With Other Entities

So far, we have seen how LLCs can outweigh the pros of both sole proprietorships and corporations. However, how does it rank against other business entities? Here is a breakdown comparing LLCs to other business entities, as it is crucial for you to keep them in mind before making your initial business decisions. I wouldn't want to skew your perception of LLCs as the only option you have, despite the fact that the theme of this book is all about LLCs. Depending on the type of business or cause you are pursuing, it is vital to stay informed about the different business entities so you can choose the right fit for you.

LLCs vs Partnerships and Limited Partnerships

Partnerships are basically an association between two or more owners wherein they legally agree to share the ownership and profits generated by the business. It shouldn't be confused with corporations, which involve many members but as shareholders. Moreover, LLCs are basically a fusion of partnerships and corporations. This is what makes LLCs versatile. Coming back to partnerships, the traditional partnership is not limited—that means it doesn't protect the owner's personal assets when exposed to business debts and other liabilities. On the other hand, limited partnerships (LP) consist of a combination of general partners who have unlimited liability (meaning their personal assets aren't protected from business liabilities) and limited partners who enjoy limited liability (their personal assets are protected from business liabilities). However, the caveat to this is that these limited partners will end up with limited control over their business. On the contrary, LLCs do have that limited liability protection to cover the members and, in addition, flexibility with management and ownership. This is what makes the LLC more appealing as a legal structure when compared to partnerships. Furthermore, I wouldn't suggest getting into a partnership unless it is with someone you trust. LLCs have that protective shield to cover your personal assets, so there is less room for you to become exposed by your members. Whereas with partnerships, if you get involved with a fraudulent partner, this can increase your risk of having your personal assets seized.

LLCs vs Cooperatives and Nonprofits

Let's now compare LLCs with cooperatives and nonprofit organizations. Cooperatives are basically businesses that are owned and managed by members, especially for community-driven causes. Members share the profit and make decisions collectively to lead the business in the direction they want to go. Nonprofits are basically nonprofit organizations that operate mainly for charitable and social purposes. You will find many nonprofits operating for causes related to education, religion, and other community-held values. When assessing both cooperatives and nonprofits, cooperatives face challenges like raising the necessary capital to survive; based on the ownership structure, you will find the limited liability aspect varies among members. When you look at nonprofits, they tend to be in a similar situation with regard to raising funds, and they often have to rely on the government for grants and donations. Nonprofits are tax-exempt in nature (meaning taxes don't apply to what they make), and their ownership structure doesn't consist of any owners or members (shareholders). Again, when you compare these two structures to LLCs, we can point out that LLCs have the advantage of limited liability, a flexible ownership and management structure, and the pass-through taxation.

LLCs vs Franchises

Lastly, let us look at franchises. A franchise is a business model where a franchisor provides an operating agreement and rights to a franchisee to operate a business using a brand's established system. For example, if you want to be an entrepreneur and have your own McDonald's franchise, then a franchisor will provide you, the franchisee, with rights to use the established brand name of McDonald's and share all the trade secrets and the operating system to run the franchise seamlessly with other McDonald's stores in the region. You will need to pay initial franchising fees and also regular royalties to the franchisor. So, why would I personally still rank the franchise below the LLC, even though it sounds interesting? It has mainly to do with control. The franchisor in this agreement will have control over the business, not you. You would be only the franchisee. On the other hand, LLCs grant you the right of ownership, and that's why LLCs eventually come out on top as the most attractive option for entrepreneurs.

What's the right business entity for you?

Now, let's bring everything we have learned together and identify the ideal entity for each business model.

Sole Proprietorship: Suitable for individual owners, especially freelancers, independent contractors, local providers, and any small business that is operated online or offline by a single person.

Partnership: Suitable for professional-based services such as law firms, accounting firms, consulting firms, medical consulting firms, engineers, and financial service-based businesses. Moreover, it can be a joint venture.

Corporation: Suitable for larger companies that are looking to attract investors through IPO/stocks. It can be startups aiming for growth potential and seeking venture capital funding.

Cooperative: Suitable for community-based initiatives and causes. These may relate to food and housing requirements, worker unions, credit unions, renewable energy, etc.

Nonprofit: Suitable for community-driven causes such as money for charity, education, religious causes, social services, health services, environmental causes, and other social causes that benefit the community rather than just the business.

Franchise: Suitable for owners who are looking to operate businesses with the help of an established brand and business model. They should be willing to give full control to the franchisor. Examples of franchise businesses include fast-food chains, retail stores, and service-based industries.

LLC: You already know that LLCs are ideal for small- to medium-sized businesses, professional services, retail, ecommerce, real estate ventures, tech startups, and even family-owned businesses.

LLC Structure: Factors to Consider

Let us look in detail at the factors to consider when deciding on an LLC structure. The two common types of LLC structures you need to know and focus on are single-member and multi-member LLCs. A single-member LLC involves a solopreneur being the only shareholder of the LLC. On the other hand, a multi-member LLC consists of two or more shareholders. There are more types, such as domestic LLCs and foreign LLCs, but I won't go into too much detail here. To define them briefly, domestic LLCs are those businesses formed within its own state where business is conducted. Whereas foreign LLCs are formed and operated in a different state than your own. For example, if you live in California but form and conduct your business in Texas, then you have a foreign LLC. Most entrepreneurs select foreign LLCs to get some kind of tax advantage, as we've discussed. The tax rates vary from state to state if you are based in the U.S.

Single-Member LLC vs Multi-Member LLC

Ownership nature

Coming back to single-member and multi-member LLCs, they are basically differentiated by the number of owners. Moreover, you will find that single-member LLCs have simplicity as an advantage when it comes to making decisions. On the other hand, multi-member LLCs require a well-drafted operating agreement to establish the decision-making process and other proceedings. What makes multi-member LLCs advantageous over single-member LLCs is that they pool the resources and capital of multiple owners, whereas single-member LLCs require that the solopreneurs pursue financing options by themselves.

Taxation

There are also some slight differences between the two when it comes to taxation that you need to know about. For instance, single-member LLCs will pay higher self-employment taxes, as they receive all the profits from the business. Whereas multi-member LLCs involve members sharing the profits and having it taxed accordingly. However, these two LLC structures both have pass-through taxation benefits.

Ownership flexibility and financing requirements

When assessing the ownership flexibility aspect, you will find it is difficult to transfer ownership with single-member LLCs. On the other hand, multi-member LLCs follow the defined operating agreement to facilitate any ownership transferability. When it comes to capital or financing requirements, it is easier for multi-member LLCs with multiple owners or investors pooling their shared capital and contributing toward the LLC.

Decision-making process

Decision-making is crucial, and single-member LLCs thrive on having complete control of their business and making decisions without any hassle or compromise. On the contrary, multi-members have that complex decision-making process that involves voting rights for making big, strategic decisions; and as it often goes with human nature, it is common that there are clashes of interest among members.

Looking into the long-term and exit strategy

If you are looking for an LLC that is made for long-term growth and vision, then multi-member LLCs are made for it, following the pros that were discussed earlier. Having shared capital, resources, and diverse ideas boosts growth and expansion. When it comes to exit strategies, multi-member LLCs also have the capacity to transfer ownership and sell off shares so the LLC can wind down without any issue, as compared to single-member LLCs.

Overall, multi-member LLCs seem to be the more attractive LLC structure if you want to focus on long-term growth and sustainability of your capital and resources. In the next section, we will go further into assessing the tax implications for these two LLC structures.

Tax Implications for LLC Structures

To close this chapter, let us dig into the tax implications for the two common LLC structures and how they can affect your financial projections.

Tax treatment

When it comes to single-member LLCs, the single owner should file Form 1040 using Schedule C and they will, by default, need to pay taxes on all the business's income when it's passed to their individual tax returns. On the other hand, multi-member LLCs need to file Form 1065 (informational tax return) to report income and expenses. Members will pay taxes on their individual tax returns. Both single-member LLCs and multi-member LLCs have the advantage of pass-through taxation, as this protects them from double taxation.

When it comes to self-employment taxes, LLC owners by default are subjected to these taxes based on the profits or losses generated by the business. In addition, they include Social Security and Medicare taxes. Keep in mind that self-employment taxes can be higher for single-member LLCs when compared to multi-members.

You may be wondering which LLC structure would require more professional tax help in order to optimize its tax efficiency. Well, let's put it this way. Tax regulations can be a complex topic, and this will depend on the LLC members' individual needs and level of knowledge and expertise. Where this is lacking, professionals are ready and willing to assist. I would always suggest hiring one if you can afford it, regardless of what structure you end up choosing. It is worth the money and removes many headaches in the long run.

Partnership Taxation or Corporate Taxation

When talking about multi-members, they have the option to be taxed as a partnership or as a corporation. The subtle difference is that if the LLC wants to be taxed as a partnership, then they have to file Form 8832 and will still benefit from pass-through taxation. Whereas, if they want to be taxed as a corporation, they have to again choose if they want to be treated as a C corp or S corp, and then file Form 8832. However, for getting taxed as an S corp, it does require meeting some eligibility criteria depending on the number of shareholders.

That's a lot of information thrown your way to help you understand more about the structure of an LLC, its significant advantages, and how each ranks against other business entities. In the next chapter, we will discuss the steps required to start forming an LLC. We're only just getting started!

Key Takeaways From This Chapter

- LLCs provide a shield that protects your personal assets from business liabilities, unlike sole proprietorships and partnerships.
- LLCs have better tax advantages and smoother decision-making processes with less formality when compared to corporations.
- LLCs offer better limited liability protection when compared to cooperatives and nonprofits. In addition, LLCs offer full control of the business, unlike franchises.
- Single-member LLCs consist of a single owner, whereas multi-member LLCs consist of multiple owners or shareholders.
- Multi-member LLCs are better than single-member LLCs when it comes to sharing financing options, lower self-employment taxes, and being tailor-made for long-term business growth and expansion.
- Single-owner LLCs should file Form 1040 using Schedule C, and multi-member LLCs should file Form 1065. They both benefit from pass-through taxation.

Chapter 3

Forming Your LLC

The way to get started is to quit talking and begin doing.

— Walt Disney

I n this chapter, we will walk you through each critical step to form your LLC. You will learn what actions to take in order to form your LLC without becoming overwhelmed by the process.

This can be intimidating for beginners, and that is why this book is designed for you. It removes the jargon and guides you through each step clearly and succinctly. This chapter will follow the steps in chronological order, so be sure to follow them diligently.

LLC Formation: A Step-by-Step Overview

Let's refresh and look at what you need to do when forming an LLC. Some of these steps will be discussed in detail in the following sections of the chapter; this section will provide you with a brief overview of the steps we're going to take.

Conduct a business name search and check availability.

The first thing you need to do is select a name for your business that is unique and will help you stand out from your competitors. It should comply with your respective state's naming requirements if you are based in the U.S. You can complete this task by heading over to the Secretary of State's site and accessing the business registration portal to conduct your business name search. You will find out whether the name is available or being used by another business.

Prepare and file the articles of organization.

The next step is to start drafting the articles of organization. This document outlines your initial statement to form an LLC within the chosen state (in the U.S.). You will find this document is very similar to the articles of incorporation. In a nutshell, it's an official document to legally certify or declare the formation of your organization. You can complete this action by filing it with your respective Secretary of State office either on paper or online.

The basic details included in the articles of organization include:

- the name of the LLC
- principal address of the LLC
- names of all the members and management
- registered agent information

Choose a registered agent and their responsibilities.

A registered agent is basically a company or an individual that will be your point of contact to receive your LLC's legal documents and official proceedings on your behalf. By default, the registered agent should reside in the state where your LLC is formed. So, if you encounter a virtual address when you look up an agent, then you should ignore it. Go with registered agents that have clearly stated a physical address and operate in your state. Moreover, your registered agent should be up to the task of accepting your essential documents and providing transparent communication during business hours—which is five days a week.

Obtain necessary business licenses and permits.

Next up, find out what business licenses and permits are mandatory to operate within your industry and business type. These can vary from state to state, so make sure to do your research first. You can complete this step by reaching out to your state (or local) authorities and asking them about all the licenses and permits you need to apply for. Write all these down and ask how you can apply for them.

Comply with state-specific requirements and regulations.

Another step in the process involves you doing more research and familiarizing yourself with your state's requirements for LLCs. For example, inquire and find out how the reporting process works, how and when to file taxes, the types of taxes and rates involved, and whether there are other compliance regulations. Speaking of taxes, it is mandatory to acquire an EIN from the IRS. This is to help you report federal taxes on a regular basis using your unique EIN tax identification.

Draft an operating agreement.

Next up, you will need to draft your operating agreement. However, it should be noted that this step is optional, as it is not required by all states if you are based in the U.S. If you are based in California, New York, Maine, and Delaware, then you will definitely need an operating agreement. Again, it is important to inquire with your respective state about whether your LLC will require an operating agreement at some point.

Open a business bank account.

The final step in the formation process is to open your business bank account for your LLC. Some states will have differing laws when it comes to requirements to start an official business bank account, but this step should be completed after you officially register your LLC.

Registering an LLC With Government Authorities

Let us now talk about registering your LLC with the appropriate government authorities. This shouldn't come across as an overwhelming step, despite some complex regulations in some states, because I'm going to explain everything you need to know in simple terms. The following are a few things you should keep in mind when registering your LLC with the government.

Understand the registration process.

It is important to note that your LLC registration will not be done at a federal level. It is always done at a state level; this is why I stressed the significance of doing research about the state you'll be doing business in and knowing the requirements and procedures involved for the formation of your

LLC. This information can be easily obtained by visiting your respective state's Secretary of State online portal and looking up the mandatory forms you'll need to apply for registration.

Understand the documentation required.

At this point, you should have access to the documents you need to fill out. The first thing that should be on top of your priority list is filling out the articles of organization. The articles of organization may be listed under different names in different states. For example, if you are based in Alabama, Washington, Texas, New Jersey, New Hampshire, Delaware, or Mississippi, then it is called the "Certificate of Formation." Moreover, if you are based in Pennsylvania, Massachusetts, Iowa, Idaho, Utah, or Connecticut, then it is known as the "Certificate of Organization." The critical details required for filling these out include your LLC's name, physical address, registered agent details, and your ownership structure and management.

Expect to wait some time for the LLC registration to process.

When it comes to the processing period for your LLC registration, this length of time will depend on the state your business is being formed in. I have seen it take as long as a month or so to finalize the registration in some states. Some states may be able to speed it up to within just a few days and have it ready for you. By speeding things up, I mean you can pay an additional fee to have it ready early.

Facilitate a smooth LLC registration process.

To expedite the entire registration process as much as possible, it is recommended that you use your online resources and platforms. It is much more convenient and faster than filling out and mailing in physical paperwork. Moreover, you can find a lot of online resources on your Secretary of State's website to find information on things such as fees and guides for filling out forms and registering your LLC.

Seek professional legal guidance.

Of course, you can always offload some of this responsibility to professional legal assistance by hiring an attorney. These professionals can give you personal guidance to ensure everything goes smoothly in your LLC formation and that you are complying with all the state laws and regulations. Some states have complex laws, so if you encounter any difficulty in understanding what needs to be done to move forward, don't hesitate to reach out for professional help.

The LLC Operating Agreement: Outlining the Details

Let's talk more about operating agreements. Though there are a few states that do not require one, it is essential to know what it is and how you can draft one. First and foremost, you need to understand why this is an important step for your LLC. An operating agreement helps you to clearly define the rights and responsibilities in your LLC ownership and management structure. Having this legally binding document on hand will also help on occasions when there is a dispute.

This document provides transparency to prevent any confusion and legally protect members from any miscommunication on their part. In addition, it outlines profit and loss distributions based on the shares each member holds, as well as their respective roles in the decision-making process.

Now, let us look at what needs to be kept in mind while drafting an operating agreement. Your draft will take into account the following factors:

- **Clarifying ownership profit distribution, voting rights, and percentages**. A critical purpose for an operating agreement is to clarify the ownership percentages of each LLC member to determine the rightful distribution of profits and losses. Moreover, voting rights indicate the power each member can hold for making big decisions in the LLC.
- **Defining management structure and decision-making**. Another critical element in your operating agreement should define the management style of your LLC. The first thing you'll decide is whether it will be member-managed (LLC members or owners have collective control of the company) or manager-managed (members delegate control to the hands of the management team). After you clarify this, you can determine how your decision-making process will look among your shareholders and organization.
- **Outlining provisions for dispute resolution**. Another important element you will need to outline in your operating agreement involves provisions for resolving potential disputes among LLC members. This can include any arbitration processes, and it can also outline the process for a member's withdrawal from the shareholder's seat.
- **Flexibility**. After first drafting your operating agreement, you may feel that any and all actions henceforth are bound to what was written down, but this is not the case. This should help remove any anxiety you may be feeling as you're drafting it.

Operating agreements can and should be reviewed regularly to make changes based on your business's growth. For example, if your company were to merge with another company, this would require updating the operating agreement. If your company is trying to survive under turmoil and adverse market conditions, then it can be reviewed and updated according to a new strategy to keep things afloat.

In a nutshell, an operating agreement is not set in stone, and you can always look to tweak it as you go about your business venture. However, it should always outline the mandatory elements as explained above to make sure there won't be any confusion and that potential disputes can be resolved with immediate effect.

Acquiring the Necessary Licenses and Permits

When it comes to obtaining the required licenses and permits for your LLC, you will need to look at the following factors and take the necessary steps to comply.

- **Do the research in advance**. When you do the research for your industry, it will be easier for you to identify the licenses and permits you need because different industries have varying requirements. For instance, a general business license is required for most businesses when they are formed. It allows you to legally operate your business in your respective state. This will cost you anywhere from $50 to $300 depending on the industry you operate in. Then there are other licenses and permits, such as the business tax ID, zoning permits, sign permits for putting up sign boards, and sales tax permits for collecting sales tax. If you run a home-based business, then you will need a home occupation license. If you are in construction, then you will need a building or construction permit. If your business is service-based and you hire many workers, you will need to acquire health permits, safety permits, and even environmental licenses. As you can see, it will vary depending on the industry you are in, and you should prepare a checklist of the necessary licenses and permits after you inquire about them.

- **Identify the federal and state regulatory bodies involved**. The next thing you need to find out is which government authorities are responsible for issuing the permits and licenses in your specific industry. Find out if they are issued by the local, state, or federal government. For example, my trucking business requires federal licenses and permits. Since our business comes under transportation and logistics, we had to acquire our licenses from the U.S. Department of Transportation. Likewise, you will need to know where you can get your licenses and permits.

- **Know your compliance obligations and renewal procedures**. After you get your permits and licenses secured, you need to fully understand the obligations involved with each of them. That means knowing how you need to conduct reporting, pay fees, and meet the deadlines associated with these permits. Additionally, you will need to have the renewal dates and procedures integrated into your work system so that you can keep your licenses updated and avoid any problems down the line.

- **Store and maintain clear documentation for your licenses and permits**. I cannot stress enough how important it is to keep everything organized within your administrative system. To avoid any legal-related challenges in the long run, you should store your licenses and permits in a safe place, along with all the necessary paperwork, forms, certificates, etc. Keep everything updated and review them frequently. You can always seek help from professionals for documentation purposes and also for legal-related questions.

Opening a Business Bank Account for Your LLC

Before wrapping up this chapter, one final step you'll need to take after registering your LLC is opening your business bank account. Opening a bank account for your LLC isn't a complicated procedure, and this will help you to separate your personal finances from your business finances. This account will also facilitate actions such as accounting, tax reporting, etc. The following are a few things you need to do when opening a bank account for your business.

- **Research suitable banking options for your LLC**. When you do your research, you will find certain banks to be more suitable for opening an account for your LLC. Some banks out there can even provide efficient services and low fees. However, I would suggest you focus on the long term and go for a bank that allows smooth online banking services for business transactions and provides accessible customer support 24/7 over banks offering low fees and less value. Some banks can offer tailor-made services for LLCs, such as providing business credit cards.

- **Know the documents and other requirements for opening a business bank account**. For LLCs, you basically need to have in hand the following three documents when opening your business account (apart from the obvious such as your ID): articles of organization, EIN, and, if required, your operating agreement. Moreover, there will be a minimum initial deposit required by most banks to open a bank account, just like our personal accounts, so you will need to have these funds ready. Furthermore, you should look to set up overdraft protection to avoid overdraft fees.

- **Maintain effective financial record-keeping**. It is important to integrate a smooth and effective financial record-keeping system into your LLC to separate your personal transactions from business transactions using your business bank account. Use reliable accounting software such as Quickbooks, Zoho, FreshBooks, and Xero—these are some of my top picks. This will help you simplify your record-keeping and also your tax reporting during tax season without much hassle.

All of the steps we've covered in this chapter will help you form your LLC without complication, as you now have all the crucial information to accomplish them correctly.

If you haven't already, add all the details you have learned in this chapter to your personal checklist so that you don't miss any critical details and to make sure you have everything sorted properly during your LLC formation. Now that you have learned all about the steps for forming an LLC, let us move on to the next chapter where you will learn how to manage and operate your LLC.

Key Takeaways From This Chapter

- The steps involved to form your LLC include undergoing a business name search, filing the articles of organization, selecting a registered agent, obtaining business licenses and permits, complying with state-specific requirements, drafting an operating agreement (not required in some states), and opening a business bank account.
- It is important to inquire and understand the registration process requirements, as these can vary from state to state. Look to utilize online resources and online applications to facilitate a smooth registration process.
- Drafting an operating agreement is required by some states, and it should include critical details such as ownership profit and distribution, voting rights, percentages, structure, decision-making processes, provisions for dispute resolution, and withdrawal conditions.
- Business licenses and permits can vary depending on your specific industry. They may be issued by the local, state, or federal government.
- Look for suitable banking options that will help you benefit from convenient banking for your business in the long run. Integrate effective record-keeping and accounting software for maintaining your financial records.

Chapter 4

Managing and Operating Your LLC

Life-fulfilling work is never about the money—when you feel true passion for something, you instinctively find ways to nurture it.

— Eileen Fisher

So far, you have learned about the basics of LLCs in terms of legal structure and the steps involved in forming them. In this chapter, you will learn more about the day-to-day operations of your LLC and how to manage it effectively.

This chapter will break down aspects such as understanding the roles and responsibilities of LLC members, first and foremost, the legal and compliance requirements that need to be met, and other factors such as effective bookkeeping practices, managing your budget, documentation, and holding meetings with your LLC members. Let us get straight to it and learn more about LLC operation and management.

Knowing the Roles and Responsibilities of LLC Members

When it comes to the roles and responsibilities of the members and managers involved in your LLC, they will largely depend on the structure. The two types are member-managed and manager-managed LLCs. We went into a little detail about these two in the previous chapter, but we're going to learn more about them in this section. The major way to distinguish these two is given in the name itself.

Member-managed LLCs are those that have members collectively participating and making decisions in the day-to-day operations; they have full control in the business's decision-making processes. This should be specified in the operating agreement when you draft it.

On the other hand, manager-managed LLCs involve members appointing managers, and this dedicated management team will oversee day-to-day operations and also have a say in business decisions. It is important to note that these managers who are appointed aren't necessarily the shareholding members of the LLC.

Let us take a look at each of the members' roles and responsibilities based on the following aspects.

Obligations and decision-making authority

Let's be clear when it comes to the members' obligations and their roles in decision-making. For instance, members in member-managed LLCs actively play a role in the management, operations, and decision-making regarding the direction they're taking the business. Their other obligations include complying with what was agreed upon in the operating agreement and participating in the voting process for making strategic business decisions and other important choices related to the company. On the other hand, members in manager-managed LLCs are more passive in nature compared to member-managed LLCs when it comes to their role in management, operations, and decision-making. Instead, the appointed managers make the decisions regarding day-to-day business operations, though members still have voting rights to make strategic business decisions and must comply with what was agreed upon in the operating agreement.

Designated managers' duties in daily operations

As you know, in manager-managed LLCs, members designate managers to lead and manage daily business operations. This can include tasks such as overseeing projects, managing finances, recruiting and letting go of employees, etc. The managers' obligations include executing decisions in the best interest of the members, and they will report to members regarding all business matters. If you do end up choosing this LLC management structure, you should be sure to clearly define the reporting nature and other communication structures in your operating agreement. Having effective communication lines between managers and the members upstairs is vital for the sustainability of the business and to ensure that the right business decisions are being made.

Addressing conflicts of interest and fiduciary responsibilities

When it comes to times of dispute, such as in conflicts of interest, it should be a practice that managers and members focus on the LLC's best interest and avoid any conflict for personal gain. Additionally, when it comes to fiduciary responsibilities (this applies mainly to manager-managed LLCs), the designated management team should always act in the best interest of the company and avoid prioritizing personal gain. For example, managers should prioritize satisfying clients' needs in the best interest of the LLC rather than prioritizing a transaction that benefits them personally. Furthermore, managers in some LLCs can have financial protection against business liabilities and expenses and can defend themselves against claims on their conduct by something known as "indemnification."

Being Compliant With Legal and Regulatory Requirements

Satisfying the initial legal requirements when forming an LLC is important. However, maintaining this compliance as you are managing your LLC year after year is another challenge. Nevertheless, you can manage this diligently with no need to sweat over it, as the compliance system is usually implemented early on after your LLC formation. You can help yourself by having a compliance team with you to make sure all legal requirements are being met and that you're fully compliant (yes, this is a real department in many top organizations).

Your success in staying compliant and not breaking any legal and regulatory requirements will depend on the following factors.

Understanding ongoing filing and reporting obligations

When you familiarize yourself with filing and reporting requirements, this can help you facilitate a smoother process. Understand the requirements at both the state and federal levels. This may include submitting annual reports, tax returns, and other filing requirements. It can vary depending on the industry you operate in, as well as state regulations.

Knowing important deadline dates and renewal requirements

It is important to keep a calendar updated with important dates, like deadlines and license renewal periods. You might also jot down the deadlines for submitting annual reports and tax returns as specified in the above point. The recurring theme here is to keep everything organized.

Understanding and complying with state-specific regulations

Familiarize yourself with your state's specific regulations. This should be right up there in your compliance organization checklist. As you now know, different states and industries have varying regulations and requirements for LLCs. Therefore, you should regularly check for any changes in regulations that could interfere with your LLC's operations.

Seeking professional guidance for assured compliance

I cannot stress enough how important it is to have a professional as your helping hand. When you find the right tax advisor, accountants, and attorneys, the money you pay them is worth it, and you will always stay updated and compliant with any local, state, and federal laws that could impact your LLC.

Implementing internal controls and processes to meet compliance standards

Besides seeking professional assistance from external sources, your internal process is what can truly define your compliance management. This should include efficient book-keeping (which we'll discuss in the next section) and execution of other administrative tasks to ensure everything is organized and that your company is in control of all compliance-related issues.

The key takeaway from this section is that you should do everything you can to stay compliant, as this is only possible when you are regularly monitoring any changes in regulations and also reviewing your current compliance system. Later on in your company's growth, we suggest hiring a Chief Compliance Officer (CCO), like my company has, to manage and ensure that your organization stays compliant with all legal and regulatory requirements.

Record-Keeping and Bookkeeping Practices for an LLC

Now, let us discuss another important business function that requires proper attention to detail as you manage your LLC or any business entity—bookkeeping. Ensuring proper record-keeping helps you stay apprised of your company's financial health, and also ensures you stay compliant with tax-related regulations.

So, as you can see, everything is interlinked, and this is what makes every top organization tick—they have efficient coordination among all departments. If one department lacks work efficacy and quality, it can have a devastating effect on the rest of the functions in the company.

Coming back to bookkeeping, let's look at a few things you need to keep in mind when you are trying to maintain accurate financial records for decades to come.

- **Establish an effective record-keeping system**. First and foremost, you need to plan it out and decide where all your financial records are going to be stored. Traditional businesses in the past had loads of physical documents to keep track of, but in modern times, we are taking everything digital. Invest in a digital platform so you can organize all your financial records systematically and access them with ease anytime you need to. For example, you could make use of high-quality accounting software brands, an ERP (Enterprise Resource Planning) system, or any cloud-based platform.
- **Document every financial transaction, contract, and agreement**. The next thing you need to do is always keep records of important financial transactions. These include receipts, invoices, purchase orders, credit card statements, and other payment records. This may also include expenses that your company is incurring regularly. Additionally, you should store important contracts and agreements, such as your office lease, supplier contracts, client contracts, and all other various contracts.
- **Make it a habit to keep track of income, expenses, and cash flow**. The three most influential accounting

terms in my books are income, expenses, and cash flow. When you really know and keep track of all three of these metrics, you are sure to lead your business in the right direction financially. Record your income, such as revenue from sales, investments, and other services. Keep an eye on your expenses, such as salaries, taxes, operating costs, and office supplies. Lastly, calculate your cash flow to monitor the cash coming in and the cash going out of your LLC.

- **Hire the right professional for effective bookkeeping**. When you invest in and hire a gem of an accountant or bookkeeper for your company, you are going to find out five to ten years later just how valuable an asset that person is to you. You should look to hire professionals to help manage your company's financial records to ensure accuracy and provide highly reliable financial reports.

It is essential to retain and safely store financial records for the long term, in case there are situations in the future where these are required by the state for auditing purposes or any legal issues. It is always advisable to be prepared for the unexpected rather than regret it later when you're not prepared.

Managing Finances and Budgeting for an LLC

Keeping financial records is crucial, but I want to go through another financial management lesson that involves managing your LLC's finances and budgeting. Treat this as a continuation of the previous section. We will look at each of the steps that can help you to track and manage your LLC's budgeting effectively.

- **Develop a comprehensive budget for your operations**. The first step you need to look at is to create a detailed budget that will define all your business's operations. For example, in a specific project, create a budget that lists your income you generate and the expenses involved. This is an example of a short-term budget, or micro-budget, and it will help you to keep track of both ongoing and future projects. A long-term budget involves keeping track of your company's overall income and creating a budget plan to maximize your LLC's profitability. This is where you need access to your business's financial data history, market analysis, and projected financial figures as you outline your detailed budgets.
- **Allocate funds for expenses, investments, and growth initiatives**. The second step is to start allocating funds to key areas. I allocate to three areas for my budget so that it is easier to allocate funds strategically—expenses, investments, and growth initiatives. Your expenses include salaries, office rent, office supplies, utilities, etc. Allocate funds for investments such as business assets, equipment, technology, and other business-related investments. Finally, set aside portions of your budget for growth initiatives that will lead to business expansion and growth. This can include better marketing initiatives, opening a new office, etc.
- **Monitor and analyze financial performance and key metrics**. The third step is to make it a habit to

monitor the company's financial performance through key metrics known as key performance indicators (KPIs). Examples of these include analyzing your income statements, cash flow statements, balance sheets, and other financial reports to calculate your company's profitability, liquidity, debts-to-equity ratio, and much more.

- **Implement effective cash flow management strategies**. Your effectiveness in managing a healthy cash flow in your LLC will come down to your daily operations. So, you will need to look internally and externally to find any gaps and challenges that may be causing cash flow issues, such as liquidity problems. Common causes could be high operating expenses, high vendor rates, fewer sales, and poor marketing; these can all affect your cash flow.

It is crucial to keep reviewing and updating your budget on a regular and frequent basis. Moreover, consider hiring the right person to manage the budgeting for you, as I suggested earlier. You can also reach out to financial advisors who can offer helpful insights into your growth opportunities, potential investment opportunities, tax season planning, and many more financial considerations.

Holding Meetings and Documenting LLC Decisions

We will wrap up this chapter by going over another important aspect of managing your LLC. This has to do with the long-term business strategic decisions that need to be made; hence I left this for last. I'm talking about holding meetings and documenting the important decisions that are produced in those meetings. It is mandatory that you host regular meetings with shareholder members as well as the managers (if you are purely a manager-managed LLC).

The following are some of the best practices to ensure you get the job done right and produce insightful and game-changing decisions to take your business forward.

- **Regularly hold meetings as per the requirement**. Firstly, you should always aim to hold regular meetings and most of the time, the details of this can be specified in your operating agreement, such as when and how many per quarter. The main goal here is to ensure that the number of meetings held is commensurate with the relevance and number of business and state requirements. The more important matters you need to solve, the more meetings you may need because, let's be real: You cannot make all the big decisions in just one round of meetings per year.
- **Set the agenda, inform participants, and record meetings**. Now, you should set up a systematic meeting ritual. It starts with informing the participants about the main goals of the meeting— this is what you will call the meeting agenda. This will outline the points to be discussed and what attendees can expect, as well as the expected outcomes. Next, notify all the participants in advance of the meeting's date, time, and venue where it will be held—these meetings can be face-to-face or virtual. Lastly, appoint a person to attend and record your meetings by tracking minutes. This is the person who will let you know if all the key topics

were covered, and they will also be the one to jot down important notes about what was discussed in these meetings.

- **Maintain a record of LLC decisions, voting results, and member approvals**. After key decisions have been made as a result of these meetings, your company should stay organized by keeping a clear record of all the decisions and actions that will impact the LLC. This may include documenting voting results, dispute resolutions, and other business-related decisions. Make it detailed by noting down the names of those who attended the meetings, their role in making the decisions, and also their official signatures they used to approve these important decisions, for formality.

- **Store meeting minutes and documents for future compliance requirements**. This goes back to earlier in the chapter about staying compliant and maintaining coordination among all business functions and departments. You will need to store all the data safely in your system so you can refer to it in the future when you need it. You may end up needing this data for compliance-related requirements, such as in situations where your business is subjected to auditing or other legal inquiries.

Every meeting should be conducted efficiently and not just for the sake of having a nice visit and chit-chat. I like my meetings to be intentional, and I don't waste anyone's time. The best advice I can give you is to invite those to the meetings who will participate and have a role to play. Moreover, follow up on your meeting decisions and push forward to take actions that can affect your business positively.

At this point, you've learned all about the steps to form an LLC and, now, how to manage it effectively. Take a moment to make sure you've digested all the key details that go into managing a real organization. The next chapter will be a bit different as we go in-depth about liability protection in the world of LLCs.

Key Takeaways From This Chapter

- Any LLC can be member-managed or manager-managed. Member-managed LLCs entail members actively participating in the company's daily operations, management, and decision-making. Whereas manager-managed LLCs involve designating managers to lead the company's daily operations, management, and decision-making, while members still play an active role in the strategic business decisions.

- Every member and manager involved in the LLC structure should know their roles, responsibilities, and obligations. These should be specified in the operating agreement, and this can include internal communication and management styles, decision-making processes, and other fiduciary responsibilities.

- Ensure your LLC stays compliant with legal and regulatory requirements by understanding the ongoing filing and reporting obligations, tracking important deadlines and renewal requirements in your database, and establishing internal processes to document records for effective compliance.

- Establish an effective record-keeping and bookkeeping system in your LLC by using a cloud-based platform or system to store records and document financial transactions, contracts, agreements, expenses, income, and cash flow to maintain accurate financial records.
- Manage your financials wisely by developing a well-defined budget for your business operations, allocating funds to the three key areas, and monitoring financial performance through KPIs to ensure the budget is being followed. Moreover, look to keep reviewing and updating your budget based on business factors.
- Hold regular meetings and document LLC decisions efficiently by setting clear agendas, monitoring minutes and key points, and documenting meeting and voting results for future use and compliance.

Chapter 5

Understanding Liability Protection

A pessimist sees the difficulty in every opportunity; an optimist sees the opportunity in every difficulty.

— Winston Churchill

We're halfway through! You have now learned the essential details of the LLC business entity, the steps involved in its formation, and how to manage the day-to-day operations involved.

In this chapter, we will look to understand better the liability protection aspect that an LLC brings to the table, as this can further reassure you regarding the legal protection of your personal assets. We will cover the concept of limited liability protection, or the corporate veil.

You will learn the differences between personal and LLC liability, how to avoid piercing the corporate veil to keep protecting your personal assets, LLC insurance coverage key points, and many risk management strategies that can help you minimize liability. Let's get into it.

Limited Liability: What Does It Mean for LLC Owners?

Before broaching liability protection, you will need to learn the theoretical definition of limited liability. Essentially, limited liability is a concept for business owners (in this case LLCs) that offers a great extent of personal asset protection. So, whenever you hear this term, you should automatically interpret it as "personal asset protection."

Going deep into this, limited liability protection is a set of legal principles that helps to protect the personal assets of LLC owners from business liabilities and debts. So, for instance, during times when your LLC faces financial challenges, such as not being able to pay creditors or even going bankrupt, the bank or creditors will not touch your or any of the LLC owners' personal assets but instead will target the LLC's assets, since the LLC is considered as a separate entity from the business owners (as we distinguished in Chapter 2).

Pretty simple, right? Limited liability is solely focused on the separation of personal and business assets, as an LLC is regarded as a separate entity from its owners. Hence, the owners' or members' personal assets remain protected. Now, let us look at a few details of limited liability protection, as there are a few personal liability exceptions. One obvious exception is a situation where there is fraudulent or otherwise unlawful activity going on that could damage any third party. Other exceptions include personal guarantees on debts or loans, or trying to personally capitalize on the LLC. A personal guarantee is basically when an individual (most likely the business owner) promises in advance to repay the loan, even after the business goes bankrupt. This essentially means that the bank or any creditor involved can personally sue the business owner even after the business defaults on the loan payment. These exceptions can break the limited liability protection shield, and the owner or member can be personally held liable for these acts.

Therefore, to avoid these unlawful acts and maintain robust personal protection, it is essential for an LLC structure to maintain compliance and adhere to regulations and laws. Some ways to ensure this include checking from the beginning whether your LLC registration and formation was conducted according to all the state law requirements and having organized systems in place, such as a business bank account, to separate your personal and business finances for efficient bookkeeping and record-keeping. Moreover, during your LLC's tenure, following all the details outlined in the operating agreement helps you to stay compliant and avoid any situation that might compromise your limited liability protection.

In a nutshell, limited liability protection is crucial for LLC owners, not only for their personal asset protection but for the best interest of their LLC, too. One big advantage of having limited liability is the freedom to attract potential investors and partners to your LLC. More and more investors will be willing to become part of your LLC, since there is limited liability protection in place that would protect their personal assets against any business liabilities. Hence, you will find LLCs are always an attractive option for external parties who want to be involved with your business and invest in it.

Personal Liability vs LLC Liability: Know the Differences

Before going deeper into the chapter, you will need to understand clearly the differences between personal liability and LLC liability. These two are distinctly different, and understanding their protection factors can help you to make the right decisions in the long run.

The clear distinction between personal liability and LLC liability

The major difference is in the protection they offer. For example, personal liability refers to the legal binding of a person to their debts, obligations, and other claims. So, in an event of financial or legal inquiries, an individual's personal assets are at risk. On the other hand, LLC liability refers to the legal responsibilities of the LLC as a separate entity. So, in the event of financial or legal inquiries, the LLC's assets are primarily at risk.

Situations where personal liability may arise

It is vital to understand when situations of personal liability may occur at any given time. Fundamentally, these arise when an individual guarantees any business debt or loan, gets involved in any fraudulent or unlawful activities to harm others, or ignores any legal responsibilities associated with them. For example, not paying your taxes or being involved in unethical activities.

LLCs can shield owners from liability

When you look at LLC liability, it offers a protective shield to the owners, placing only the LLC's assets at risk. If your LLC is structured properly and operating as per the guidelines defined in your operating agreement, your members will definitely be protected from any business-related legal claims, obligations, or debts, and their personal assets will remain untouched.

We can better understand the significance of LLC liability protection by going through a few real-life case studies. One common liability case involves products where there are manufacturing defects, design defects, or anything that can harm consumers. This is known as product liability, and an LLC can be sued for this.

In real life, we have seen many LLCs and also corporations with limited liability protection suffer from this. Philip Morris (now Altria Group Inc.) was sued by a woman who had lung cancer in 2002, as she claimed their cigarettes had put her in that situation and Philip Morris had failed to warn her about the risks of smoking. As a result, Philip Morris was sued for product liability and after appealing the case, had to pay around $28 million.

Another company that was sued for product liability was General Motors in 2008. Their lawsuit stated that a damaging chemical was used in its Dex-Cool coolant and as a result, caused engine damage and a lot of leaks. This was filed by about 35 million customers for around $150 million. In both of these scenarios, the businesses were held liable and the owners' assets were protected.

This is where you can see how an LLC provides protection for members. Therefore, it is important to adhere to legal and ethical business practices to ensure there is balance in separating personal and business liabilities and also to avoid illegal activities that could lead to piercing the corporate veil.

Piercing the Corporate Veil: How to Protect Your Personal Assets

You've already been introduced to the term "corporate veil," as I mentioned it briefly earlier in this book. It is basically the wall or protective shield separating your personal life from your business life. This essentially acts as a barrier to protect your personal assets from business liabilities. Piercing the corporate veil is a legal term that refers to an action wherein the separation of an individual's personal assets from the business entity is broken or "pierced." Thus, it refers to the individual becoming personally liable for business debts or obligations.

The idea of lifting the corporate veil

I wanted to cover this in part because, even though LLCs offer protection of the owner's or member's personal assets, there are possible legal events where all of that could go to dust. The court can treat the LLC business as an extension of the owner, hence providing an opportunity to hold the owners personally liable for any business debts and other legal claims. In such cases, the corporate veil, or the wall that acts as the barrier, would be disregarded.

Factors that could lead to piercing the corporate veil

Now, you may be wondering how this can happen. There are some factors that can lead to such a situation, and common ones include the following:

- **Fraud**: Undoubtedly, being involved in any fraudulent activities, unlawful transactions, or misrepresentations.

- **Undercapitalization**: When there is inadequate capitalization in your business, which leads to not meeting your business's financial obligations.
- **Commingling of assets**: When you mix your personal assets with your business assets and funds.
- **Ignoring formalities**: Not properly adhering to your legal responsibilities and formalities as outlined in your operating agreement and according to state requirements.

As a result, these factors can pierce the corporate veil and leave you exposed and the owners and members personally held liable for their and the business's actions.

Best practices to avoid piercing the veil

To avoid any piercing of the corporate veil, it is best to take actions and incorporate some best practices for prevention. Here are some common practices your business should incorporate to help you avoid making mistakes and finding yourself in one of the previously mentioned scenarios:

- **Maintain sufficient capitalization**: Make sure your LLC has adequate capitalization in order to meet any financial and legal obligations.
- **Separate finances**: Ensure your personal and business finances are separated at all times and accounted for in financial records separately. This includes avoiding any commingling of assets.
- **Adhere to formalities**: Ensure that you follow all the specified formalities according to your state and operating agreement, and take actions to adhere to them.

- **Document and maintain records**: It is crucial to have an effective documentation system to record all your business transactions and also to store records safely for later use against legal claims, as we discussed under the compliance management section.

Strategies for protecting personal assets in case of lawsuits

In the event of veil piercing and your personal assets being exposed in lawsuits, you can take actions now to protect them in advance. Consider investing in asset protection tools to protect your personal assets. Examples of these include family limited partnerships and trusts. Moreover, purchasing liability insurance can help to protect your personal assets against legal obligations and claims. You will learn more about insurance coverage in the following section.

Seek legal guidance to safeguard personal assets

Ultimately, you will want to turn your attention to seeking professional help and guidance from experts, such as your business attorneys, to ensure compliance and avoid missing something that could be deemed unlawful. A good practice is to establish a legal review system where you and your legal experts (attorneys or advisors) review the business's practices regularly to identify any flaws in the system that might expose you and your business to legal claims.

Evaluating Proper Insurance Coverage for Your LLC

Being found liable in legal claims can be a stressful situation. However, having liability insurance—insurance that helps cover any legal fees should your business be found liable for harm to third parties—can help you protect your business and personal assets from various liability claims.

When you have proper insurance coverage for your LLC, it can help mitigate risks against liabilities. To understand more and know what actions you can take to incorporate insurance coverage for your business, take a look at the following three steps.

- **Step 1**: **Evaluate insurance needs based on the nature of your LLC's operations**. First up, you will need to assess your LLC and the industry you operate in. Conduct a risk assessment to identify any risks of potential liabilities in your operations and the effects those would have on your consumers. In the case studies from earlier in the chapter, we discussed companies like Philip Morris and General Motors, which were involved in product liability cases; this can happen in your industry as well. Assess your industry risks, your business structure, and the nature of your services or products, and then you will have a clearer idea of your insurance coverage needs.
- **Step 2**: **Understand the different types of insurance policies**. The next step is to educate yourself on the various insurance policies that are

relevant to LLCs. Insurance includes coverage for the following:

1. General liability: This insurance will cover any property damage, injuries, and other legal expenses.
2. Property: This insurance specifically covers any property damage, equipment damage, or accidents or theft involving your assets.
3. Workers' compensation: This insurance provides coverage for workers' or employees' medical expenses or paid leave in the event of accidents in the workplace.
4. Professional liability: This insurance protects you against professional errors, negligence, or mistakes.
5. Business interruption: This insurance covers any lost income and pending expenses in the event of your business being temporarily unable to operate and shut down.
6. Cyber liability: This insurance covers any damages related to cyberattacks, potential data privacy violations, and data breaches.

- **Step 3**: **Prioritize insurance policies based on your business's needs**. Knowing the types of insurance policies as described above can help you prepare for any unexpected events after you evaluate your industry risks and your business's insurance requirements. You won't need to buy all these insurance policies. For example, if you are a solopreneur with zero employees, you wouldn't need workers' compensation insurance coverage, or if you are conducting your business online and function without a physical office, then you wouldn't need property insurance.

General liability insurance is non-negotiable, as it can prove to be essential for most businesses out there. It can be your all-round coverage to protect your business against any third-party damages, such as property damage, unethical advertising, personal injuries, etc.

Professional liability insurance is optional, as it is for specific industries—mainly service-based industries—that offer a lot of professional services. This insurance coverage can cover claims for any negligence or errors while providing your professional services. You will find law firms, medical firms, and other professional services taking professional liability coverage.

Additionally, you should consider consulting with professionals in the insurance industry, such as your insurance brokers, to make sure you understand all the pros and cons involved in these coverage options and also to customize these policies to suit your business's requirements.

Risk Management Strategies for Minimizing Liability

We will wrap up this chapter by going through risk management strategies that you can implement to minimize liability. Minimizing liability in any business is a great risk management practice to safeguard your LLC. You can plan an effective risk management practice by following these steps:

Conduct risk assessments to identify potential hazards and vulnerabilities.

First and foremost, carry out your risk analysis by assessing your ongoing LLC work processes and operations. Moreover, consider all the external factors that could pose a threat for your organization. You can divide your risk assessment findings into two categories—internal and external. Internal are purely risks you find within your business operations that could be a potential vulnerability, such as safety in the workplace, the level of data security, and even your financial transactions (whether your expenses outweigh your income, for instance). External factors are things outside your organization that you have no control over but can pose a threat, such as inflation, government intervention, economic downturn, etc.

Implement risk mitigation measures and preventive controls.

The bitter truth about risk management is that you cannot ever eliminate 100% of the risk. There will always be a minute fraction of risk involved in any business, even if you do an excellent job minimizing it. That is why no one talks about eliminating risk, rather they say let's mitigate them; it's purely about damage control and trying to prevent the worst-case scenario. Your risk mitigation measures should look to implement protocols that can help reduce the risk involved. For example, suppose you have data security challenges. This may require cybersecurity practices that can help you secure your data and reduce the risks of data leaks or other fraudulent activities. Other risk management measures will involve what you implement internally in your LLC. For example, here are some effective measures:

- Training employees: Educating your staff about the significance of risk management and implementing ideal practices and compliance measures can create an efficient risk-management work culture.
- Insurance: As we learned in the previous section, if you invest in liability insurance plans, like your general liability, property damage, workers' compensation, etc., this can help to cover damages in the long run.
- Documenting processes: Implement a mantra stating that everything your business interacts with, be it within the organization or outside of it, should be documented. This will ensure that you have documented proof should you have to face any legal claims or compliance-related matters in the future.

Develop emergency response and business continuity plans.

It is wise to expect the unexpected. This is why developing emergency contingency plans for rare and high-magnitude situations, such as data breaches, disruptions in business operations, or even natural calamities, should be of the highest importance. As an entrepreneur, you must take this seriously, as there could be a day when all that was accomplished through hard work and commitment could be lost due to external factors you could not control. The best we entrepreneurs can do is account for the possible emergency situations and devise plans designed to mitigate the risks of those situations happening or otherwise limit the possible damages should those events occur.

Incorporate legal and safety compliance practices into daily operations.

Another way to mitigate risks is correlated to the lessons we have learned so far—one in particular—and that is *compliance*. If your LLC adheres to all legal regulations and has an effective compliance system in place, then you are going to mitigate risks quite smoothly compared to other competitors in your industry. Hence, being organized and communicating clear organizational policies and guidelines for ethical business transactions and adhering to the state laws will help your business remain relatively immune to risks.

Regularly review and update risk management strategies to adapt to changing circumstances.

Last but not least, you should review your risk management measures and assess vulnerabilities inside and outside your LLC on a regular basis. It is a continual process, and you and your team should stay on alert to identify potential risks and adapt to changes in a dynamic market.

Following these risk management practices will help not only your business to keep thriving under difficult business conditions but also your corporate veil to remain intact at all times. Even though LLCs have a protective shield in protecting members' and owners' personal assets, this is not always a guarantee, as we've seen.

This chapter has helped you understand how the corporate veil can be pierced and the measures you can take to prevent this from happening to your LLC. The next chapter will give you some more information about staying immune to corporate veil piercing—we are going to talk about taxes.

Key Takeaways From This Chapter

- Limited liability essentially means that a business owner's personal and business assets are separated. It ensures that their personal assets are protected against business liabilities and other obligations.
- There is a clear distinction between personal liability and LLC liability. In the event of legal enquiries and other obligations, third parties will hold the individual legally responsible with personal liability measures in place. Whereas the LLC as a separate entity will be held legally responsible against debts, obligations, etc., if an LLC liability measure is in place.
- Piercing the corporate veil is a term used to describe when the protective wall separating business assets from personal assets is disregarded for one reason or another. Once the veil is pierced, it means an individual's personal assets will be at risk regarding business debts and obligations.
- Ensuring proper insurance coverage for your LLC helps you to minimize liability. Some common insurance policies include general liability, property coverage, workers' compensation coverage, professional liability insurance, and business interruption coverage.
- Risk management is a continual process, and you and your team must regularly work to identify potential vulnerabilities both internally and externally, and then implement risk management practices to mitigate them.

Chapter 6

Taxation for LLCs

Paying tax is not a punishment. It's a responsibility.

— Chris Matthews

We could not complete any business book without covering taxes. It is simply unavoidable. And to lead a business legitimately, it is crucial that you understand the basics of taxation involved in your LLC.

You know a little bit about pass-through taxation, which means that your LLC won't be taxed at a federal level but will instead "pass through" the profits/losses to an individual's tax return. However, there are many other things you need to learn regarding the topic of taxes.

This chapter will walk you through the different tax treatments for an LLC, such as pass-through taxation, partnership tax treatment, corporation tax treatment, filing requirements, deductible expenses, and also strategies for minimizing taxes for your LLC. Let's dive straight in.

Understanding Tax Treatment Options

LLC tax treatment based on the number of members

It is essential to understand the tax treatment of LLCs, and this can depend on the number of members. For example, you are already aware of single-member LLCs and multi-member LLCs. Now, let us look at the tax treatments for both.

In a single-member LLC, the owner should file a personal tax return by using Schedule C and report their business's income and expenses. By default, the owner ends up paying self-employment taxes on the entire net income generated. So, if you are the owner of a single-member LLC, and your company generated a net income of $75,000, then you must pay your tax rate on that $75,000.

On the other hand, in a multi-member LLC, it is regarded as a partnership under the tax law. Instead of using Schedule C, each member uses Schedule K-1 to report their share of the business's profits (or losses), and then they report that on their personal tax returns. For example, if you are a shareholder who owns 41% of your multi-member LLC, and your business generates a net income of $75,000, then you will need to pay the tax rate on the share of profits you receive from that $75,000. In a nutshell, you can see that multi-member LLCs have to elect for partnership taxation as a means to avoid double taxation, and their members will report their respective shares of the business's income plus deductions on their individual tax returns.

Considering eligibility for corporate taxation for an LLC

We know that LLCs can utilize a default pass-through taxation feature, but they can also elect to be taxed as a default corporation. You have already learned that corporations exist as two types—C corps and S corps. If the LLC was to elect to be taxed as a C corporation, then they would be exposed to double taxation. That means the LLC will pay taxes on the business's profits and also on the dividends distributed to individual tax returns. On the other hand, if an LLC elects to be taxed as an S corporation, they will utilize the default pass-through taxation but can avoid self-employment taxes on some portions of their business. To go deeper into this, you will need to understand the tax requirements for S corporations and meet criteria, such as having a limited number of shareholders and also specific classes of stock.

So, what are the benefits and drawbacks of different tax treatments?

For an overview, let us compare each tax treatment and look at their advantages and disadvantages. For pass-through taxation, it is quite a simple taxation treatment where individuals avoid double taxation but have to pay self-employment taxes.

For partnership taxation (which is treated for multi-member LLCs), they can pay lower self-employment taxes based on the profit distribution and also benefit from pass-through taxation. However, the filing process can be complex compared to the pass-through tax treatment of a single-member LLC.

When looking at C corp tax treatment, the benefits of that include corporate deductions. However, individuals can be subjected to double taxation. Meanwhile, an S corp benefits from pass-through taxation and a reduction in self-employment taxes on some part of the net income. But the drawbacks include complex eligibility criteria and other limitations.

Hopefully, this gives you the gist of the different tax treatments, and now you know that with your LLC, you do have different tax treatment options you can take advantage of based on your LLC structure and what treatment will benefit you the most based on your business or personal finance goals.

The choice is yours, and you can choose the ideal treatment based on your specific circumstances. Nevertheless, it is best to consult with tax professionals, such as your tax consultants, advisors, or accountants, to know for sure what the most favorable tax status is for your specific LLC. Have a good talk with your tax professional and understand the tax implications involved in each to make a collective decision regarding the right tax treatment.

Filing Requirements for LLCs

Now, let us look at the necessary tax filing requirements for your LLC. This is crucial in order to stay compliant with respective local, state, and federal regulations, as you should always be paying the right amount in taxes. Here are a few things you need to keep in mind while learning about your LLC's filing requirements.

Identifying essential tax forms and Schedules for LLCs

I will be brief and straight to the point, since I've already mentioned this a few times in the book. For a single-member LLC, you need to report your LLC's income and expenses using Schedule C. This will be part of your personal Form 1040. Whereas, for multi-member LLCs, since it is part of the partnership tax treatment, each member should use their Schedule K-1 and file Form 1065, outlining their respective shares of the business's profits or losses.

Understanding local, state, and federal tax filing obligations

It is important to refresh your memory on your government authority's tax filing requirements and obligations. For instance, your LLC can be subjected to federal income tax reporting. Moreover, some LLCs will have state and local tax reporting obligations, such as reporting income taxes and sales taxes, and this can purely depend on the state you operate in and even the nature of your business and industry.

Disclosing income, deductions, and credits on the appropriate forms

The next thing you need to understand is what you need to disclose on your tax filing forms. In brief, there are three things you need to report—income, deductions, and credits. Your business income includes your sales and other avenues that generate revenue for your business. All these go under income, and all the sources should be reported as part of your LLC's income. Deductions include your business expenses, like employee salaries, operating costs, office rent, utilities, and other expenses related to the business's operation. Lastly, credits, or "tax credit," is the amount that you as a taxpayer can deduct from the taxes you owe. This can be applied as a state "discount" in some cases.

Knowing filing deadlines and extensions for LLC tax returns

When talking about the dates for filing your LLC tax returns, this can vary slightly depending on the LLC structure. For instance, for single-member LLCs, since they need to comply with the individual income tax return filing, the deadline is usually the 15th of April. Whereas for multi-member LLCs, since they use the partnership tax treatment, their deadline to file taxes is by the 15th of March following the tax year. When it comes to extensions, you can request to push it back to the 15th of September of the same year.

Importance of accurate and timely tax reporting

Though you can request extensions to file taxes, it should be your top priority to file taxes by the deadlines to avoid any sort of penalty for filing late. Your reputation with the IRS will matter in the long run. Moreover, accurately reporting your income, associated deductions, and credits is mandatory if you want to avoid having your LLC audited or penalized. Hence, having a certified accountant on staff to take care of this would be a great investment that I'd highly recommend.

Identifying Deductible Expenses for an LLC

So far, we have covered what you need to report your LLC's income and pay taxes according to the shares you hold (if you are with a multi-member LLC). However, you need to also report your deductions in order to minimize your tax obligations. So what are the different types of deductible expenses you can report for your LLC?

Common deductible expenses for LLCs

Ideally, these are the common deductible expenses for LLCs that you can report in your tax filing on a regular basis. These should be documented and accounted for accurately while you manage your business:

1. **Business expenses:** These include costs incurred directly from any business operations, such as utilities, rents, equipment, etc.
2. **Employee salaries**: These include wages, salaries, IRA contributions, health insurance, and other employee benefits.
3. **Travel:** All expenses related to traveling for business purposes or to meet clients are deductible.
4. **Meals:** All expenses related to meals while on these travels are deductible.
5. **Marketing**: These include expenses for carrying out marketing campaigns, advertising, and any promotional-related initiatives.
6. **Depreciation and amortization**: You can deduct the cost of your business assets through depreciation and amortization.
7. **Professional services:** These are particular fees paid to professionals, such as accountants, attorneys, consultants, or to any other service-based professionals. Yes, they are deductible, too.

The above list provides you with the expenses you can deduct, and it is recommended that you keep track of these accurately for when you are ready to file your LLC tax return.

Categorize expenses into cost classes

To make things easier for you when filing your deductible expenses, we suggest categorizing your expenses into three major parts—operational, marketing, and administrative.

- **Operational costs:** Includes your daily operations expenses for running your business. So, this is where your rent, utilities, office supplies, and other related expenses can be categorized.
- **Marketing costs:** Includes your advertising expenses, like marketing materials, web development, events, or any other costs related to your business's marketing.
- **Administrative costs:** This will include general business expenses to manage your LLC, such as office equipment, insurance premium payments, employee wages and salaries, and other administrative expenses.

Categorizing my expenses into these three categories helped me out massively when it was time to report deductible expenses during tax filing.

Criteria for determining the deductibility of specific expenses

There are three specific criteria for ensuring that specific expenses can be classed as deductible. They are as follows:

- **It should be ordinary**: Expenses should be necessary for your business and clearly implied in your daily business operations. It should be an ordinary expense for running your business operations. Any cost that is not related to running your business isn't deductible. For example, buying a gaming console for entertainment purposes.

- **It should be directly related**: These particular expenses should have a direct relation or connection to the income you produce in your business. For example, if your equipment has a direct connection to producing income for your company, then it meets the criteria.

- **It must be substantiated**: Deductible expenses should have accurate documentation in order to prove the authenticity of these expenses. This is why I mentioned that all your expenses should be accounted for accurately through effective bookkeeping and record-keeping.

Depreciation and amortization of assets for tax purposes

You can deduct expenses related to depreciation and amortization of your business assets. But what are they, exactly?

Depreciation refers to your tangible assets that lose value over time. This can include the equipment you use for business purposes, such as your computers, or the property, such as your warehouse or office. With depreciation, you can subtract the asset's cost depending on its lifetime use. On the other hand, amortization refers to your intangible assets losing their value over time. Your intangible assets in this case might include copyrights, patents, trademarks, etc.

Knowing that all these expenses are deductible is crucial, but tracking them and keeping good records of them is even more vital. As usual, I would urge you to hire tax professionals or have a reliable accountant on staff to keep track of and identify all your deductible expenses. Document these effectively, and you can claim all your deductions correctly to optimize your tax efficiency.

Exploring Strategies for Minimizing Taxes for Your LLC

Minimizing your taxes is every LLC owner's dream. In fact, I wouldn't be wrong to say that it is any taxpayer's dream as well. Is it possible to minimize your taxes, after all? Yes, it is, but it requires strategic planning and accounting for certain factors.

Hence, we will wrap up the chapter by going through a few strategies that you can utilize to minimize your taxes and optimize your tax efficiency.

Utilize tax planning techniques to optimize the LLC's tax position

Ensuring that you have efficient tax planning in place can help your LLC's tax position in the long run. But what are the different tax planning techniques you can use? You should have a plan for this from the beginning of your LLC journey, and your options might include the following techniques:

- **Choosing the favorable entity type**: After doing your research and understanding the tax implications of various business entity types, such as single-member/multi-member LLCs, and also the tax treatments of partnerships and corporations, you will understand how to choose the most favorable one to reduce your tax liabilities.
- **S Corp tax classification**: The best strategy to reduce your tax liability lies in the tax treatment you

receive as an S corporation. If your LLC is eligible for it, elect to be taxed as an S corp to receive the benefits of paying lower self-employment taxes while still avoiding double taxation in the process.

- **Income splitting**: A phenomenon called income splitting involves distribution of income among members of a multi-member LLC in order to balance their tax brackets. Income splitting can help to minimize the LLC's overall tax liability significantly.

- **Timing your deductions**: Another strategic move you can implement is related to your deductions. For instance, try to time your deductions based on the tax year, increasing expenses into the current tax year and delaying income that is coming through into the following year. This will maximize your tax efficiency and help you to pay lower taxes.

Tax credits and incentives available to LLCs

It can be beneficial to explore your tax credits. For instance, research and identify at a federal and state level all the tax credits applicable to your business's nature and the industry you operate in. Additionally, find out about possible incentives, such as energy efficiency or R&D credits that may be applicable to some businesses.

Incorporate tax-saving strategies into your LLC's financial and operational decisions

There are a few more tax-saving strategies that you can incorporate into your LLC's internal decision-making processes to see long-term benefits. These include investing in retirement plans, such as IRAs and 401(k)s for you and your employees. This will provide you with tax-deferred advantages. You can also open Health Savings Accounts (HSAs) if your LLC is eligible. You would deduct contributions to this account and use the tax-free funds for any medical-related expenses.

Moreover, contributions to charitable organizations can be considered as deductions under various tax laws in most states if you are based in the U.S. Furthermore, look into taking advantage of tax deductions on the depreciation of business property; use Section 179 of the IRC to identify business properties that qualify.

Before wrapping up this chapter regarding taxation, I want to emphasize the importance of seeking guidance and regularly reviewing your LLC's business processes and financial statements with your accountant and tax advisors in order to capitalize on tax-saving opportunities.

I have a routine process in place for this because it can be quite complex in the trucking industry. Regularly reviewing the tax regulations and our business's work processes helps us find opportunities to save on taxes. We practice the timing strategy by accelerating trucking expenses in the tax year and deferring trucking-related income.

I hope this information will be valuable to you regarding the sometimes intimidating subject of taxes. It can be complex, but with the right information and guidance, you will have it down in no time. We will continue on the topic of financial management in the next chapter.

Key Takeaways From This Chapter

- There are various tax treatment options available for LLCs. This will depend on their structure as a single-member LLC or a multi-member LLC. Multi-member LLCs are treated as a partnership. Also, LLCs can be taxed as a C corporation or an S corporation (if eligible).

- Depending on the elected tax treatment, LLCs will need to file depending on this classification. For example, single-member LLCs use Schedule C to file tax obligations, whereas members in a multi-member LLC use Schedule K-1.

- Deductible expenses can help you minimize tax liability. Common deductible expenses include business operating expenses, salaries, advertising and marketing, depreciation and amortization, fees paid for professional services, and travel and meal expenses for business purposes.

- Deductible expenses can be categorized into three different cost classes, and it should meet three criteria to be considered deductible—the expense should be ordinary, it should be directly related to business income, and it should be substantiated.

- You can maximize your tax efficiency by using tax planning techniques such as choosing the favorable business entity, income splitting, timing deductions, and if eligible, opting for the S corp tax classification.

Chapter 7

Financing Your LLC

Business opportunities are like buses: there's always another one coming.

— *Richard Branson*

unding your LLC is an essential topic now that we've discussed how this element can be a potential con in our comparisons of advantages versus disadvantages in the earlier chapters. This is because there are a few challenges that LLC owners can face when it comes to financing their LLC to sustain their business compared to corporations, for example.

In this chapter, you are going to learn more about the financing options you have at your disposal for funding your LLC. We will explore both self-funding and external financing options.

You will learn more about loans, grants, and alternative financing sources. Moreover, by the end of the chapter, you will know how to identify and attract potential investors that can fund your LLC by drafting a compelling pitch.

On top of that, you will also gain insights on how to manage your cash flow in order to stay financially healthy and see positive growth in your business.

Exploring Options for Funding Your Startup

When you initiate your LLC startup, the funding you'll need to get going, especially in the first few years, is crucial. You'll need to seriously consider various options to make sure your business will have adequate financial resources and backing to stay up and running and avoid legal or financial issues.

For that, you'll need a comprehensive breakdown of your options, and luckily, despite the LLC's challenging aspect of funding, we can guide you to acquiring this essential financial backing through the following sources.

Personal savings or assets

Your first source or option will be to look at your personal savings. Even if you are not a fan of the idea of using your own personal finances, it should still be considered as a backup option at the very least. But if you have adequate savings which don't interfere with your personal life and financial goals, then feel free to allocate a portion of your savings to your business's startup costs. The advantage of using your personal savings is that it completely removes any debt or liability factor, and no interest need be paid because you are borrowing the money from yourself. However, like I mentioned before, if it interferes with your personal life and financial goals, this could be a bad decision for you. On the other hand, you could also explore other personal assets, such as your property. Consider a home equity loan to help you allocate funds to your LLC business.

Loans from family, friends, or personal contacts

If the first option isn't applicable to your circumstances, then you will have to explore the loan route. But before approaching any banks, you should consider asking for loans from your family members, close friends, or other personal contacts. Family and friends can provide you with more flexible loan repayment terms compared to banks, but beware of causing rifts in relationships should you fail to treat the agreement with respect or pay according to those established terms. In other words, approach this route with caution. If you dive deep into your personal or business contacts and find someone who takes an interest and wants to be part of your project, you may be able to get loans from them or even ask them to be a sponsor for your business. A pro tip I would suggest here when taking loans this way is to draft a promissory note. This is basically a document that outlines your loan's specific terms and the repayment deadlines, and also clarifies the interest rates. It is better to have a promissory note as an official document for accountability rather than just promising someone verbally that you'll pay them back at some point.

Grants and government programs for small businesses

Another option you should consider is researching the local, state, or federal grants which are available to small businesses. The SBA (Small Business Administration) provides specific loan programs for small businesses at favorable repayment terms. You can research how to meet the eligibility criteria and read the guidelines to understand the entire application process.

Crowdfunding and online platforms for raising capital

Crowdfunding is basically the process of raising funds from a big pool of investors or individual sponsors in exchange for early incentives or rewards. You see crowdfunding as a major funding source nowadays, especially in the real estate industry. If your business plan and proposal is exciting and can attract the eyes of many individuals, people will be willing to give a small amount toward raising capital for your business. You can find crowdfunding platforms online; a few big ones include GoFundMe, StartEngine, Indiegogo, Kickstarter, and SeedInvest.

So, what's the best option for you?

There is no perfect option, to say the least, and it will all depend on you. Your individual circumstances, the nature of your business, the amount of capital you need to raise, and many other factors will influence your decision. In some cases, it may be a good idea to use two or more sources in order to raise the capital you need for your business. However, before you choose, let's summarize the pros and cons of each funding option. If you decide to go with your personal savings or assets, the positive thing here is you are not taking on debt, but you are also depleting your personal financial resources. Taking loans from your family and friends can provide you with flexible repayment terms but can also take a toll on your personal relationships with them. The big advantage of grants and government programs is that you receive longer repayment terms, but it can be a bit complicated to satisfy the eligibility criteria for them, and the application process can take a lot of your time. And finally, crowdfunding can help you raise capital from a broader audience—especially if you use online platforms. That's what I like about this option, but it isn't as simple as you think. The challenge is that there is no guarantee that you will get enough investors or sponsors who are interested in funding a business that hasn't proved its potential yet. Understand all your funding options and make a wise decision. Choose the right one for you based on your circumstances and the nature of your business.

Self-Funding vs External Financing: Pros and Cons

The above section provided you with several funding options, but you should fully understand the nature of the two approaches at your disposal. Self-funding is where you access funds from your personal resources and finances. External financing is accessing funds from external parties, such as through family, friends, crowdfunding, banks, etc. This section will provide a brief overview of the positives and negatives of each.

Pros of self-funding

I think it is easy to understand that if you do choose the option of self-funding, you basically keep full control of your capital and your business operations. This is an independent route that removes the headache of relying on investors or other lenders. You do not incur any debt and you don't pay any interest, so this can be a financially stable route if you have adequate funds. You'll save a lot of money by not having to pay interest, specifically. It is your money, so you make the rules. You will have a flexible timeline for injecting funds into your business whenever you think it is necessary without having to beg anyone else. In a nutshell, this is the most straightforward and cost-efficient route.

Cons of self-funding

Now, despite the advantages available with self-funding, it isn't for everyone. If you have limited financial resources or assets, this can be a bad option for you. You won't be able to fund your business adequately, and it can hinder your business operations and the potential for it to scale and grow. Moreover, it can put you at personal risk regarding your personal financial resources if your business fails. That is something I would be wary of, especially if your financial resources are limited, and I would urge you not to opt for this option.

Pros of external financing

External financing removes any limitations when it comes to accessing a broader audience and raising more capital for your business. This can help you fund your business operations regularly, and it provides an option to quickly scale and grow your LLC without affecting any of your personal financial resources. In addition, in some cases, you could find investors that turn out to be meaningful connections who want to invest in your business. So, let's say you are starting a business as a pet shelter, and you attract an investor that has expertise in this particular industry. It is going to help you in the long run when they share valuable industry knowledge with you and provide many insights for scaling your business. Think about the possibilities that can come with opting for this route to finance your LLC.

Cons of external financing

Of course, not every option is perfect, and there are a couple of disadvantages related to external financing. A prominent one is that you will have a lack of control over the financing of your business. Ultimately, it is the investors' or the lenders' decision whether to be involved and regularly fund your business. If there is an event where they decide to part ways, you will lose your major funding source for your business, and that could hurt your business operations significantly. That's one thing you should be aware of, even though you could also end up attracting a well-respected investor. Moreover, another obvious con to external financing is that it involves interest payments and repayment terms, and it can also affect the profitability of your business. Involving yourself in negotiating, pitching your business plan, and drafting contract agreements can be a lengthy process as well.

Finding the right balance between self-funding and external financing

Now that you are aware of the pros and cons of each option, it is important to find the appropriate balance between the two funding approaches for your LLC. It is always important that you understand the risks involved. Self-funding involves a lot of personal finance risk if your business fails. Whereas external financing can reduce personal risk. On the other hand, external financing can involve a lot of new debt, interest payments, and in some cases, equity financing, where you share profits with investors. In a nutshell, you should base your decision on three factors:

- personal financial circumstances
- growth and expansion requirements
- willingness to split the profits and delegate control

Consider these three factors carefully when assessing your financing options, and you may find that you want a mix of self-funding and external financing. You only need to balance the percentages. I would suggest leaning toward a higher percentage of external financing (especially as a startup) so that your personal finances aren't affected. After a while, when your business has grown to a healthy and profitable level, you can start using more of your own funds if you want to bring back more control with financing.

Understanding Loans, Grants, and Alternative Financing Sources

In this section, let us look briefly at loans, grants, and other financing sources. After understanding more about them, you can add these sources to your list of funding options to create a broader foundation on which to base your decisions regarding financing in both the short and long term.

Business Loans

There are several different kinds of business loans, so it is essential that you familiarize yourself with the options available to you. Here are the common ones along with a brief explanation of each:

- Term loans: The default type of business loan where you get cash up front and you repay it with interest over a specific period.
- SBA loans: The SBA guarantees these loans, which are provided by other banks. These come with longer and more favorable repayment terms, anywhere between seven and twenty-five years.

- Business lines of credit: You get access to funds by opening a credit line, and you pay interest only when you withdraw the funds within your credit limit.
- Equipment financing: Loans that aid you in financing equipment for your business.
- Personal loans: Applicable for startups, you can take out personal loans mainly for business purposes.
- Microloan: These are offered by nonprofits or other specific lenders where you can receive as little as $50,000 to kickstart your new business.
- Invoice factoring: This can help you get your unpaid client invoices paid in advance when you collaborate with a factoring company.

When borrowing loans, you will need to think from the perspective of lenders. They look for important details, such as your creditworthiness, your business plan, projected cash flow, and in some cases, collateral. Trying to get a favorable repayment term can be vital, and your business plan can be your pitch to help you win those terms.

Grants

Government grants and funding programs are another funding source you can look at. You will find government agencies at both a federal and state level that provide monetary support to specific industries and to businesses that mainly thrive in community development. Hence, you find a lot of nonprofits acquiring these types of grants. However, it may benefit you to explore government grants and funding programs for small businesses and research the eligibility criteria, essential document requirements, and deadlines for submitting these applications. The biggest con when it comes to grants or government-backed funding is that it can be very competitive when it comes to getting your application approved, and it is not always easy to satisfy the eligibility criteria, as I've mentioned. Nevertheless, having a presentable business plan that outlines all your financial projections and how your LLC will benefit the community can help you to win over some of these government agencies.

Angel Investors and Venture Capitalists

Another alternative financing source you can look at is attracting angel investors and venture capitalists to your business project. Angel investors are those individuals who are keen on finding promising business startups. They will provide the essential funding in return for equity (or some shares) in your business. On the other hand, the nature of venture capitalists is as an investment first, and they can back you with sufficient capital for your startup. How do you win over these investors or investing companies? You need to think from their perspective. Angel investors or venture capitalists will study your business plan and its potential to grow. They care about their return on investment—they want to be reasonably sure that they will make money by providing you with money. Therefore, if you can illustrate in your business plan your company's long-term potential and forecast healthy financial projections, you will have a high probability of convincing investors. In the next section, we will go more in-depth about this.

How to Attract Investors for Your LLC

Let us go deeper into attracting investors for your LLC. If you can convince angel investors or venture capitalists to provide the necessary funding to your business, this can be a great achievement for you, as you will receive monetary support to grow and scale your business at a much quicker pace. Therefore, I will provide you with a step-by-step guide for how to attract investors to your LLC.

- **Step 1: Identify potential investors and understand their investment criteria**. The first step is all about research. By doing a simple Google search, attending industry networking events, or even diving deep into your personal or business connections, you can identify a few investors or venture capitalists who have a good track record of providing capital for startups. However, the names don't matter nearly as much as what they can do for you and whether you will be a good fit for each other. Understand their funding reliability and know what type of business models they usually invest in (if your business aligns with this, then go for it and approach the investors). Familiarize yourself with the sectors they are interested in, their risk tolerance level, and also the size of investments they usually go for.

- **Step 2: Develop an investor pitch and presentation materials**. The second step is to develop an investor pitch, otherwise known as the "elevator pitch." This will basically summarize what your business is all about, the value proposition or unique selling point your business provides, and its long-term growth potential. These three components should be present in your investor pitch, whether you write it out or verbally present it. Moreover, preparing a presentation can help you look professional and come across as a serious entrepreneur in the eyes of the investors. In your presentation, focus on succinctly outlining your business model, the market research findings, the competitive analysis, your company's financial projections, and also your ownership and management structure.

- **Step 3: Craft a compelling business story and value proposition**. The first two steps above are the most basic things you need to do, and you should be able to easily complete these steps after reading this book. Now, the third step is something different. This step is about standing out among other business startup projects and providing the "wow" factor to the investor or venture capitalists you are trying to convince. You can achieve this by presenting a business story: you narrate your business's journey, highlight the problem in the market you are trying to fix, and then talk about how you are going to provide value by introducing your solution. Try to be as passionate as possible when telling your business's story. In addition, present your value proposition—basically a unique value that your business can offer and how it will help you stand out against your competitors.

- **Step 4: Negotiate terms and conditions with potential investors**. The fourth step is to negotiate terms with the investors. By this point, you will have either convinced the investor with your compelling business story or been turned down. Regardless, you have to lay out your terms for them, and this can also win or lose the deal. In this step, evaluate your business's value by incorporating your findings from market research and your company's financial projections. Lastly, make it clear what you will offer in exchange for the investor's capital—whether this is equity (a share in the business), debt that will be repaid with interest, or any other terms that will be a win-win for both you and the investor.

- **Step 5: Address legal and regulatory considerations**. The last step is to look up certain regulations to make sure you are in legal compliance when carrying out this deal. For instance, depending on the investor you are approaching, there are some situations where you would be required to address SEC (Securities and Exchange Commission) regulations. Moreover, you will need to have legal documents ready and also be ready to state the legal and regulatory terms that both parties will comply with after an agreement is made.

Approaching investors and convincing them shouldn't be a daunting task. You can't please everyone, and there will certainly be a few rejections, but you can still find the right fit for your business by looking for someone that you personally connect with and that will promote a healthy business relationship.

To optimize your chances of convincing investors, remember to be transparent (no lying or hiding important details), be more data-driven, focus on the return on investment your business can bring to the investor, and always look to connect on a personal level. Have warm conversations, be professional, and conduct yourself with the mindset of helping both parties succeed rather than focusing only on your personal gain.

Managing Cash Flow and Initiating Healthy Financial Projections

We will conclude this chapter by briefly going through how you can manage cash flow and maintain a healthy financial status to keep the promises you've made to your investors and also to meet your desired business goals.

Develop a cash flow forecast and budget.

For your LLC, it is important to have a projection of expected cash flow (an outline of cash inflows and outflows) over certain time periods so that you can identify periods when you are likely to make more revenue or suffer potential short-comings. Having a budget in place can help you track your actual financial performance against your budgeted projections.

Monitor and manage income and expenses.

As mentioned in the earlier chapters, keeping constant track of your income and expenses and identifying how to increase income and reduce redundant expenses can help your business to maintain healthy profitability.

Implement strategies to improve cash flow.

You must take action whenever it is necessary and implement strategies to improve your cash flow. This might include assessing your internal processes. For example, assess your invoicing terms and find out if you are urging your clients to pay within a short time period so that your income is consistent each month. Implement a system that sends your clients reminders for payments and also manages your receivables securely. Moreover, when it comes to your suppliers, look to negotiate bargain prices if you can do so without harming your business relationship with them.

Analyze financial statements and KPIs.

Keep monitoring and reviewing your financial statements, like your income statements, cash flow statements, and balance sheets, to keep track of your business's financial position in the market. Utilize KPIs to track this and ensure your cash flow is sustained. For example, assess your inventory turnover, working capital ratios, etc.

Of course, seeking out professional financial advice and hiring the best financial professionals for your team can help you maintain healthy cash flow in the long run. As long as you regularly review your financial statements, budget, and metrics, and also ensure your projections are being either met or surpassed, this will help you keep a buffer of funds to fill in any future cash flow gaps.

In the next chapter, we will learn more about the contracts and agreements that will be required for your LLC.

Key Takeaways From This Chapter

- Options for funding your LLC startup include self-funding options, which include: personal savings or assets; loans from family, friends, or personal contacts; grants and government programs; crowdfunding; and, attracting investors.
- Self-funding can help you avoid debt but can also deplete your personal financial resources. On the other hand, external financing incurs debt but can help you grow your LLC quicker.

- The different types of business loans include term loans, SBA loans, business lines of credit, personal loans, equipment financing, invoice factoring, and microloans.
- Angel investors are individuals who provide funding for your business in exchange for equity (mainly). Whereas venture capitalists are investing firms that provide your business with sufficient capital.
- You can attract potential investors by researching the right type of investor for your business, developing a compelling investor pitch, presenting your business's story, negotiating terms and conditions, and providing your financial projections.
- Maintain a positive cash flow over time in your business by assessing receivables and invoicing terms, increasing income, reducing expenses, and reviewing financial statements and KPIs regularly.

Chapter 8

Contracts and Legal Agreements

A verbal contract isn't worth the paper it's written on.

— Samuel Goldwyn

L et's move on to contracts. It is essential to understand the significance of contracts whether your business is an LLC, corporation, partnership, or even sole proprietorship; there are going to be a lot of contracts involved.

This chapter will provide insights on the role of contracts for an LLC, the common types you should know about, and how you can draft contract terms and clauses as well as handle contract disputes efficiently.

The Role of Contracts in LLC Operations

Contracts will play an essential role in an LLC's operation. Some important characteristics include the following:

- **Contracts define rights and obligations**. Contracts are made to clearly outline the rights and roles of all parties involved to ensure that everyone will comply with the terms. Transparency is important when you outline obligations, such as scope of work and other conditions, should a dispute arise in the future.
- **Contracts provide legal protection and enforceability**. Contracts are there to form legally binding agreements between parties. Hence, it can provide legal protection for those who adhere to the terms and will cause issues for those who fail to meet their obligations as outlined in the contract.
- **Keep written contracts for record-keeping and clarity**. Contracts are in written form and are considered official records to be documented. If there are any disputes in the future, these contracts will be referred to in order to resolve them. Contracts should always be in written form and not verbally made because a written contract will provide proof of agreement and can be used as clear evidence.
- **Contract review and negotiation**. Contracts are also there to be reviewed regularly. Many mistakes could get through if the contract is drafted but then not reviewed on a regular basis. You need to account for any changes or variability in circumstances that may necessitate an adjustment of terms, as these should always be aligned with your business's goals and best interests. Negotiating the contract regularly will help you address any concerns and make the necessary modifications to the terms and conditions to satisfy all requirements.

The Common Types of Contracts for an LLC

Now, let us explore the various contracts used in LLC operations. LLCs need to have a guarantee for legal protection and the smooth functioning of business operations. Contracts are there to restrict or limit any incidents that could interrupt these operations at any point in time.

A few mandatory contracts you should have in your LLC's arsenal include: operating agreements, supplier contracts, customer contracts, employee contracts, and even NDAs (non-disclosure agreements). Let us look at each of them in depth.

Operating agreements and their role in defining LLC structure and member relationship

You already know the importance of having an operating agreement, as it has been mentioned many times in the book, so I will discuss it briefly here. It outlines your internal management structure, business operations, and also the relationship of each member. Everyone will be clear on their roles and obligations within the LLC, as well as other aspects such as the profit distribution, voting rights, and dispute resolution practices.

Vendor or supplier contracts for procuring goods and services

For LLCs or any other type of business, having vendors and suppliers in place to provide goods and services is essential for growth. Hence, your supplier or vendor contracts should include details such as the goods/services to be provided and the quantity; a list of deliverables and the schedule for delivering them; the pricing and payment terms; and, many other things such as warranties and contract termination resolutions. Having all these key details established and figured out will help both you and the supplier to fulfill obligations and also avoid any disputes.

Client or customer contracts for conducting business transactions

As the supplier or vendor yourself, you will need a contract for your clients or customers. These contracts will illustrate how your business will provide the goods/services, the scope of work, pricing and payment terms, delivery schedule, etc. Having these in place will help you to build trust and rapport with your clients as you draft contracts that outline both parties' roles and obligations clearly.

Employee contracts, non-disclosure agreements, and non-compete agreements

For your employees and other staff members, having a well-defined employee contract will be necessary. This should cover basic components, such as the employee's job role, responsibilities, obligations, compensation, working hours, incentives, benefits, and terms and conditions in the event of termination of the work contract. In addition, you should include non-disclosure agreements that will be signed by the employee. NDAs help to ensure that your employees don't share confidential information about your business with external parties. Furthermore, non-compete agreements are there to restrict your employees from competing with your LLC business within a certain time period after they leave your company (yes, this is a real thing).

Drafting and Negotiating Contracts Effectively

Now that you have a basic foundation about the essential contracts you need for your LLC operations, let us explore some more tips for drafting and negotiating contracts effectively. Some of the important tips I can give you include the following:

- **Understand the key elements of a basic contract**. This includes having the essential details present, such as the contract's subject matter, various terms and conditions, considerations involved, and also the signatures of the parties involved.
- **Create clear and concise terms**. Making everything clear in your contracts is mandatory. No fluff, no beating around the bush—just be straightforward and concise with your points. Define clearly all the critical details, including each parties' responsibilities, rights, obligations, payment terms, the contract termination process, and so on.
- **Identify potential risks and liabilities**. As an entrepreneur, you should tell your management team to always be on the lookout for potential risks and liabilities that might be involved with a specific contract. Always try to visualize scenarios where someone might fail to meet their obligations, as this can help you understand the level of risk involved and also devise remedies to mitigate such risks.
- **Negotiate favorable terms and protections**. Always prioritize negotiating terms and benefits that

are in your LLC's best interest. Negotiation is where you will either win or lose out on favorable contract conditions. The best way to go about this is to have your business's vision and goals imprinted in your brain so that you will know what terms will be most favorable for your business while conducting face-to-face, real-time negotiation.

- **Seek legal assistance for complex contracts**. For the above contracts that were mentioned, it can be easy to draft these yourself. However, for complex contracts, such as contracts for your asset protection, equipment, and more, you will need legal professionals who know the relevant laws well to help you draft and maintain them.

In a nutshell, ensure that your contracts are well documented and clearly communicated to all parties involved. In addition, regularly review them so that you can revise if required and modify particular terms and conditions.

Understanding Key Contract Terms and Clauses

Let us learn more about other specific contract terms and clauses you will need to be familiar with as you draft your LLC-based contracts. This will be brief, but we will cover all the essentials that should be present in your contracts.

Mandatory contract terms

In any contract, not just LLC-related ones, it should consist of three essential terms:

- Offer: A proposal made by one party to another.

- Acceptance: The agreement by the receiving party to the proposal.
- Consideration: The value exchanged between the parties involved. For example, payment, goods/services, etc.

Common clauses

A clause is a very specific legal provision that goes deep into a specific point in a contract. The three types of common clauses you should familiarize yourself with include the following:

- Termination clause: This particular clause will outline how and under which conditions the contract will be terminated or ended by either party. This can include details such as the reasons that can lead to contract termination, compensation for terminating the contract, notice periods, etc.
- Dispute resolution clause: This clause will outline how certain disputes will be resolved. For example, disputes can be resolved through mediation, arbitration, or litigation.
- Indemnification clause: This specific clause will outline the compensation one party will owe for another's losses, liabilities, or damages, and this should be specified over a certain time period.

Intellectual property ownership and licensing clauses

You will need to address your intellectual property (IP) ownership and licensing clauses in your contract as well. For instance, your IP clause will outline the intellectual property created or involved for the duration of that contract. Moreover, a licensing clause will specify the terms and conditions under which a specific party will provide permissions and rights to the other party to use their IP, which can include trademarks, patents, trade secrets, and copyrights.

Liability limitations and warranty provisions

A liability limitation is a clause that can be set to hold a specific party liable for any damages or losses over a specified time period within the duration of that contract. Whereas a warranty provision is a clause that will specify the performance and quality of certain goods and services provided by one party.

The significance of including clauses

If you still aren't sure of how important it is to include these clauses in specific contracts you draft, then let me share with you the consequences you can suffer if they are missing. This happens a lot in real life. For instance, agreeing to complex projects with a specific vendor can carry a lot of risk. Suppose you enter a contract with a SaaS business that agrees to develop an app for your business operations. If they fail to meet your requirements, this can be a huge waste of time and financial resources. Hence, if you're smart, you'll include a termination clause that outlines a 90-day milestone review, so if your business isn't seeing any development and there is a failure to meet certain milestones, then your business has the right to terminate the contract with prior notice. Let's say you're working with another business on complex projects that carry a risk of exposing certain trade secrets and intellectual property with third parties. To safeguard your business against this risk, you will include clauses such as IP ownership, liability limitation, and even dispute resolution so that you are prepared in the case of a catastrophic event.

Enforcing LLC Contracts and Dispute Resolution Mechanisms

We will wrap up this chapter by discussing the significance of enforcing contracts and implementing dispute resolution mechanisms. The previous section provided good examples of situations where including clauses can help you to avoid detrimental consequences in certain situations. It is just as important to include dispute resolution mechanisms in your contracts as well.

Contract enforcement and breach remedies

To define the term more clearly, contract enforcement means that one is ensuring that the terms and conditions agreed upon in a contract are being met throughout the course of the contract's duration. If a specific party is in breach of contract, the other party can utilize certain remedies. But what are these, exactly? It depends on the situation. Let's say you entered into a contract with a specific party and this party damages some equipment of yours. The resolution here may be that they have to compensate you for the damages and the breach of contract. If a party fails to fulfill their obligations when they enter into a contract, according to the specific performance clause, this can result in a court order for the party that is in breach. Depending on the nature of the business transaction, there can be a clause known as "rescission and restitution." This clause will restore both parties to their original positions if or when either party cancels the contract. A common example of this is a clause stating that money will be returned after a transaction if there is a contract breach.

Litigation for resolving contract disputes

Litigation, otherwise more commonly known as a lawsuit, is the legal action of taking someone to court to address and resolve disputes. Litigation will be a major part of your dispute resolution strategy; however, it is important to understand the pros and cons of this should you end up having to take someone to court to settle a dispute.

One of the advantages includes participating in a playing field where there are established rules, laws, and systemized procedures to reliably and fairly resolve matters. The court order is simple. You have a judge or jury that will decide on a verdict, and there will be evidence provided in order for them to reach their decision.

A disadvantage of litigation is that it can be costly to take someone to court, so your business might not get much out of it—especially if it is for a simple dispute. The entire process of taking someone to court and getting a verdict is lengthy, too. Taking someone to court means likely destroying that business or personal relationship; moreover, you are giving rights to a judge or jury to decide the outcome, which removes all the control you have in this situation to resolve the dispute.

What are the potential alternatives to litigation?

You may be wondering if there are alternatives to litigation after reading about all that is implied by this process. The answer is yes, and there are two in particular—arbitration and mediation. Arbitration is a very simple process where two parties present their perspectives to a neutral third party, known as the arbitrator, and this entity will make the legally binding decision. It is a much cheaper, faster, and more private dispute resolution strategy compared to litigation.

On the other hand, mediation involves a mediator who helps the involved parties find common ground and reach an acceptable resolution. This is not a legal process, and it can be advantageous for your business to consider these alternatives first before making the decision to take someone to court.

Other solutions for contract breaches or disputes

Whenever a contract breach occurs, it can be vital to seek legal advice as your first step. This can help you better understand the situation you are in and also assess the right actions you can take. Hence, having a legal professional by your side can help you protect your LLC's interests and move toward favorable outcomes in disputes. Review all contracts periodically to ensure they are in compliance with updated laws and regulations, and also modify clauses and terms that can help you mitigate potential business risks. It is critical to stay up-to-date at all times.

This chapter has provided an important legal lesson. As always, I recommend having a designated department of compliance officers and legal professionals to help you as you grow and scale your business.

Speaking of scaling, the next chapter will be an exciting one as we cover some strategies you can use to grow your LLC business to its maximum potential.

Key Takeaways From This Chapter

- The role of a contract is to define rights and obligations as well as provide legal protection and enforceability. It should be written, documented properly, and clearly communicated to all parties.

- The common types of contracts for your LLC operations include operating agreements, supplier contracts, client contracts, employee contracts, non-disclosure agreements, and non-compete agreements.
- Draft effective contracts by including the key elements: make the terms and conditions clear and concise, assess the potential risks and liabilities in contractual agreements, and negotiate for favorable terms for your business.
- Key contract terms should be included in all contracts, including the offer, acceptance, and consideration. The most common clauses include termination, indemnification, dispute resolution, intellectual property ownership, licensing provisions, liability limitations, and warranty.
- Enforcing contracts is essential for upholding the terms as agreed upon. If a breach occurs by either party, a resolution can be reached through litigation, arbitration, or mediation.

Chapter 9

Scaling and Growing Your LLC

You can focus on things that are barriers or you can focus on scaling the wall or redefining the problem.

— Tim Cook

S
o far, you have learned all about the essential steps to form your LLC and manage your business operations, and you've also been introduced to the importance of getting your taxes and contracts right. This chapter will also be an important one for you, and it is a special one to me.

You see, as entrepreneurs, it's arguable that the beginning is the easy part, where we get a business started and achieve those initial goals we set up for ourselves. When we reach a point where everything is going good and our businesses are making a lot of money, this is statistically where most downfalls begin. I will explain why.

Many entrepreneurs get so satisfied with having a sustainable business and making a decent amount of money that they fall into the trap of the "comfort owner." In this stage, the entrepreneur stops thinking about the future, as their growth mindset has diminished, and they don't take the necessary steps to make their business grow.

Luckily for you, this chapter is all about knowing how to take the necessary steps to scale and grow your LLC. Regardless of how well you may *think* your business is doing, there is always room for improvement. When you implement growth strategies and expand your business, this can help you to multiply your revenue by five times or more, and also sustain you in a competitive market.

This chapter will teach you how to develop a long-term growth strategy for your business through hiring and managing employees, expanding into new markets, and optimizing your marketing and sales strategies for scalable growth. Let's dive straight in.

Develop a Growth Strategy for Your LLC

The major foundation you need to have as a growth-mindset entrepreneur is to think about the future and assess your possibilities for growth. For that, you will need to devise a growth strategy for your LLC to grow at a rate you never thought possible. Follow these steps carefully, and you will soon be well on your way:

- **Step 1: Define growth objectives and long-term vision**. Firstly, plan what you want to achieve in the long-term. If you initially set a goal to achieve $1 million in revenue within the first three years and achieved that, it doesn't mean you stop there. You need to now develop your growth objectives. You need to now look into making $5 million in revenue in the next three years, for example, then repeat this process by making incremental moves. It should be all about progressive thinking. Your growth strategy doesn't need to be about increasing revenue alone. It can be about expanding into new locations/markets, having more employees, or optimizing your products and services. It can be anything, but it depends on your core values as a business and what your long-term vision is.

- **Step 2: Assess market opportunities and the competitive landscape**. The next step is to assess your market by conducting thorough analyses, including researching market trends, new players entering the market, your target market's interests and habits, and much more. If you find gaps, such as a new pain point that none of your competitors are solving, then you have an opportunity to provide the products/services to fill that gap.

- **Step 3: Identify key success factors and growth drivers**. By using your insights and market findings from Step 2, you can organize and determine the key factors that can help you to take your LLC to the next level. For example, if you consider the idea of filling gaps in the market, that means your growth driver will be to develop an innovative product or service to solve a new pain point; this can put your LLC at the top of the market. Moreover, you can also devise growth strategies, such as implementing unique marketing campaigns or orienting your business operations toward delivering satisfaction to clients to onboard more customers at a faster rate.

- **Step 4: Analyze potential risks and challenges**. Regardless of how ambitious you want to be, growth can be hindered by a lot of potential risks and challenges. Hence, your job is to also analyze these challenges. They may come in the form of more competition entering the market, forcing prices down, or it might be a change in the laws and regulations that threatens to hinder your business growth or financial resources. To be aware and ready for unexpected challenges, always look to develop plans to counter these events and mitigate risks. For example, to safeguard against a sudden lack of financial resources, prioritize external financing. To survive a change in regulations within your state of operation, be ready to expand into another state with more lenient regulations.
- **Step 5: Create a strategic roadmap**. The fifth and last step is to create a well-defined strategic roadmap that specifies the necessary steps your business needs to take in order to accomplish the growth objectives you defined in Step 1. Break it down into simple and manageable action plans, and use your team and resources efficiently to achieve your goals within a specific amount of time. For example, a strategic roadmap for increasing your revenue could be product development, implementing unique marketing campaigns, sales team training, modifications to current customer service process, hiring better people for management positions, and so on.

Make it a habit to keep measuring the progress of your roadmap to make sure you are on track to achieving your growth objectives. Good organizations are flexible and can adapt their growth strategy to unexpected changes in the market, so that's another important point to note when growing and scaling your LLC.

Hire and Manage Employees to Grow Your LLC

Now that you have the steps to develop a growth strategy, it's time to invest in your resources to achieve them. Your employees are the greatest resource you have, and having effective human resource management in your company is crucial for long-term growth. In this section, I will provide another step-by-step guide you can follow to hire and manage employees for a growing LLC.

- **Step 1: Understand legal and regulatory requirements**. This might sound surprising at first, but the best way to start optimizing your employee base for growth is to assess the legal and regulatory requirements in your state or country. Crucial factors such as minimum wage requirements, employee contracts, tax treatment, working hours, and health and safety laws can vary from state to state and country to country. Therefore, you need to do your research and stay up-to-date.
- **Step 2: Create job descriptions**. Now, let us get into the hiring part. Your job description is where you will win and recruit the right talent for your business. I have seen many businesses fail to be transparent in this step. Most don't reveal the package they can offer, don't define the job responsibilities well, and don't provide good insight into their company's culture and vision. As a result,

HR managers waste a lot of time talking to candidates who aren't a good fit. A big component of this lack of transparency is the salary. Think about it: If you don't clearly state the salary you are offering, you are going to get a lot of candidates who will ask for more, and you won't be able to meet those requests. This wastes time for both parties. Hence, be transparent with your job descriptions and outline clearly the job role, responsibilities, and qualifications required, as well as details about the compensation, expectations, and culture of your company. The latter is important because it will help you to recruit people who will fit in comfortably.

- **Step 3: Recruitment**. Next up, it's time to start recruiting. Implement a process that will make it easy for you to screen candidates and talk to the ones who fit your profile. Advertise your job openings across social media and the many job portals. Then, when you are contacted by interested candidates, review the resumes first and shortlist those who fit your requirements. Then you'll start to conduct interviews. You can initiate the process with a telephone interview first to confirm that they are who their profile says they are, and then schedule a face-to-face or video call meeting.

- **Step 4: Implement onboarding and training programs**. The next step is to implement onboarding and training programs for your new employees. This will help them integrate into your company culture and also make them feel at home. In this step, you should develop onboarding programs that communicate your business's core values to your new employees, as well as the policies and expectations involved in their job role. Good training programs will help them develop the skills they'll need to be successful.

- **Step 5: Establish performance evaluation systems and career development**. The best organizations measure their employees' performance to ensure they are keeping the best talent and helping to improve those who have potential and are coachable; likewise, they will let go of those who simply don't contribute to the company's success. Ensure that you are providing a feedback system that is constructive and encourages your employees to push themselves. Keep training or mentoring them so that they can excel in their careers as well.

- **Step 6: Build a positive company culture and foster engagement**. The sixth and last step is to encourage a positive working environment and a culture that is aligned with your business's core values. You want to promote a feeling of togetherness and open communication. Gone are the days of dictatorship or autocratic leadership. Thriving organizations excel with a more participative approach, with leaders putting their faith in their employees' ability to make decisions rather than micromanaging them. To cultivate this positive work culture, implement regular team-building activities so that everyone learns to work with one another and also develops a sense of belonging to the company.

Expand Into New Markets and Locations

Another important action plan you can make to scale and grow your business is expanding into new markets and geographical locations. This can help to expose your business to new markets and favorable conditions that can increase the profitability of your LLC. Moreover, if you are a business that wants to grow and be well-known throughout the nation or the world, then this section is for you. Follow these steps to implement an effective market entry strategy for scaling your LLC:

- **Step 1: Conduct market research for expansion**. Indeed, the first step always involves doing thorough research, and here, you should try to identify whether there is potential for you to expand your business. For example, our trucking business wanted to expand our logistics department by using refrigerator trucks. We saw the potential for it to increase our revenue, and the demand for transporting refrigerated goods was our driving factor. However, the state we operated in had restrictions on using refrigerated trucks. When we explored another location, we found that the restrictions there were more lenient, and we identified favorable conditions to run and manage our refrigerated trucks there. This was the expansion opportunity we were looking for, and we found it by researching the market trends, customer requirements, and also our competitors. We ended up expanding our trucking business for the first time to this new location, and we soon increased not only our revenue by utilizing refrigerated trucks but also our other trucking services.

- **Step 2: Assess the feasibility of new market entry**. It is important to also assess the feasibility of entering new markets after you've identified a potential opportunity. You will need to look at factors that are favorable to your business to make that move, such as whether the infrastructure will meet your business model functioning and that the laws and regulations won't hinder your business operations, as well as whether you can hire talent to create a strong network of vendors and suppliers to assist you on a day-to-day basis. Assess any potential risks, which can be economic or political, and any other external factors to develop contingency plans to mitigate these risks.
- **Step 3: Develop market entry strategies**. The third step is to devise your market entry action plan. This will depend on the type of business you are running and how you want to go about it. You can open up another shop or office in this new location, for starters. Or you might explore other market entry strategies, such as outsourcing your operations to the new market, getting involved in joint ventures or acquisitions, creating subsidiaries in the new location, or even licensing or franchising.
- **Step 4: Understand legal, cultural, and operational challenges**. This step will depend on how broadly you want to expand your business. If you are based in the U.S. and want to expand to a national level, then familiarize yourself with the local and state laws and regulations. This will help you get an idea of the

compliance requirements and how they will impact your business operations. Moreover, if you want to expand to an international level, it is crucial to research and understand the laws of each country, the country's culture, and how you can strategize your marketing toward enticing these new customers. You'll also need to be clear on the operational requirements that could make or break your business operations there.

- **Step 5: Establish strategic partnerships or alliances**. The last step I want to add is that working with local partners in the new location can help facilitate that market entry process and make things much smoother. Having good business relationships with local partners and vendors can help you in the long run. They will provide you with lots of people to assist in your business and make your new location feel like home. Don't be shy—reach out to local companies that can help you with your distribution channels and provide insights on how to ease your business into a new market you are not yet familiar with.

Implement Effective Marketing and Sales Strategies

Another important aspect that needs to be covered in this chapter on scaling your business is related to your marketing and sales. If you want to increase your revenue significantly and also create a loyal customer base, then you need to have solid marketing and sales strategies in place. This next step-by-step guide is mostly focused on the marketing aspect, but I believe both marketing and sales work together. Having an effective marketing strategy helps your sales team to close deals and onboard clients much easier when compared to a company with a poor marketing strategy, no matter how many talented sales professionals they might have on staff. You have to attract the attention of interested and qualified customers before closing them.

- **Step 1: Create a comprehensive marketing plan**. The first step is to create a marketing plan that outlines all the essential details, such as your market goals, budget, and detailed marketing tactics. Having this in place helps your marketing team to stick to the plan and target the right people so they're not wasting resources.

- **Step 2: Identify target markets and customer segments**. The next step is to thoroughly define your target market. This entails breaking down the market into customer segments based on key factors, such as demographics and psychographics. For example, if you are a business that offers pet food delivery, then your specific target audience might include male or female pet owners who are busy with work and don't have time to go out and buy food for their pets. You have identified the type of customers you need to target as well as the pain point that fits the solution you are offering.

- **Step 3: Develop branding and messaging strategies**. The effectiveness of your marketing strategy will depend not only on the goals, budget, or the right target market you reach out to but also the intentional branding strategy you use through your marketing messages. A general rule of thumb to stand out as a brand is to incorporate your business's core values, address the target market's main pain point, and introduce how your product/service solves that problem and is unique.

- **Step 4: Leverage digital marketing channels and social media**. In this digital age, leveraging digital channels such as search engines, email, social media platforms, and other online channels to help you reach a broader target audience is a must. Utilize the power of the digital algorithm to have your content, advertising campaigns, and other marketing messages go viral and reach the right clients.

- **Step 5: Monitor and measure your marketing performance**. The next step is to regularly monitor and measure your marketing campaigns to see if you're meeting your marketing goals. Utilize KPIs to analyze your performance and also identify potential limitations and areas for improvement.

When it comes to marketing and sales, you need to make your messages personal to see better conversion. Incorporate a mix of both online and offline marketing to help you reach out to a broader network and also diversify your marketing channel outreach. Remember to always take into consideration the latest market trends and optimize your marketing messages for better effectiveness.

These are just some of the ways you can grow and scale your LLC, and now you have a few comprehensive step-by-step guides that you can refer to any time when you are ready to scale your business. Down the line, you'll be ready to consider your options for succession planning and exiting, but we will cover this in-depth in Chapter 11.

Key Takeaways From This Chapter

- Develop a growth strategy for your LLC by defining your growth objectives and long-term vision, assessing the market opportunities, identifying key growth drivers, potential risks and challenges, and creating a strategic roadmap for achieving your growth objectives.

- Hire and manage employees for your growing LLC by understanding the legal and regulatory requirements first, then creating detailed job descriptions. Implement an efficient recruitment process, execute onboarding and training programs for new employees, establish a performance evaluation system, and foster a positive company work culture.

- You can expand into new markets and locations by conducting thorough market research to identify expansion opportunities and assessing the feasibility of entering that new market. Develop your market entry strategy by understanding the legal, cultural, and operational challenges associated with the new market, and also establishing strategic partnerships or alliances to facilitate the process.

- Implement effective marketing and sales strategies by creating a marketing plan, identifying the right target market, developing branding and messaging strategies, leveraging digital marketing channels, and constantly monitoring and measuring your marketing performance to adapt accordingly.

Chapter 10

Risk Management and Compliance

If you don't invest in risk management, it doesn't matter what business you're in, it's a risky business.

— Gary Cohn

I n this chapter, we will go into more detail about the significance of risk management and compliance for your LLC. We touched on this topic briefly in the earlier chapters, but in this chapter, we will look at the key areas and actions you need to take to mitigate business risks and stay compliant at all times when managing your LLC. Let's get into it.

Identifying and Assessing Business Risks

Undoubtedly, all businesses will have risks associated with them. For this, you need to implement a systematic risk management process to comprehensively identify business risks and devise risk-mitigation solutions. Here are a few things you need to pay attention to:

Conducting a comprehensive risk assessment

Carry out an efficient risk assessment and evaluate the potential risks or challenges that can hinder your business operations and growth. These can be anything, and they can affect any aspect of your business. For example, it might be high supplier costs that are hindering your procurement processes and thus affecting your business operations. Or it might be a lack of internal financial resources that is keeping you from investing in research and development programs to develop innovative products/services to boost revenue.

Identifying internal and external risks

When you assess risks, the best way to categorize them is based on where they are found. The two types include internal risks and external risks. Internal risks are those challenges you spot internally, such as data security issues, gaps in your business operations, less-skilled employees, high employee turnover, and so on. On the other hand, external risks happen outside your business, and these are usually out of your control. They can include challenges such as changes in legal and regulatory systems, economic downturns, market trend fluctuations, new and better competitors entering the market, natural disasters, political instability, wars, and much more.

Analyzing the probability and potential consequences of each risk

An important thing you can do after assessing and identifying each risk is to analyze their probability and potential consequences. For example, you could identify the risk of high supplier costs hindering your business's profitability by 20% and the potential consequences of keeping these same suppliers. Moreover, in this case, there may be a high probability of this happening because these transactions are part of your daily business, and you need the supplier's products to cater to the ever-increasing demands from your clients. So, you have assessed in this particular situation that the probability is high, and you've identified the potential consequence that your business's expenses will increase by 15%. As a result, you will see a decrease in your business's profitability. You would then repeat this analysis process for each business risk you identify.

Developing risk mitigation strategies and contingency plans

To mitigate risks, you need to implement strategies and contingency plans to reduce the spread and consequences they could bring to your business. For our previous example, a risk mitigation strategy could be to find alternative suppliers that offer cheaper prices but provide the same value. Your contingency plan may be to implement a screening process to identify better suppliers and also use people on your team to negotiate for a more favorable rate.

Implementing risk management practices

As the latter part of the previous point suggested, you need to incorporate practices into your business operations to ensure that you can mitigate risks and avoid suffering from harsh consequences. Have a risk assessment and management team in place as you grow, and they will be responsible for continually assessing risks and implementing practices to reduce them.

Ensuring Compliance With Laws and Regulations

Compliance with laws and regulations is an essential part of ensuring that your business stays profitable and safeguarded under liability protection, as we learned about in earlier chapters. So, how can you ensure compliance with your legal regulations?

Recognize the legal and regulatory environment

Firstly, you need to understand clearly the legal and regulatory environment that your LLC business operates in. Analyze the market and be thorough with local, state, and federal laws related to your type of business and the industry you are in.

Identify industry-specific laws and standards

Familiarize yourself with all the relevant laws, standards, and regulations specific to your industry because various sectors have different compliance requirements. Be sure you understand each law, such as the health and safety regulations in a workplace, and data privacy laws, to name a few.

Create rules and processes for compliance

After you have done your research and know your industry-specific laws, then it is time to implement rules, policies, and compliance processes for your LLC. For example, to address data privacy laws, you can implement data protection and cybersecurity measures. Or for addressing health and safety in the workplace, you can work to foster a positive working culture and a healthy working environment.

Carry out frequent auditing and evaluations

After implementing compliance strategies, your job doesn't end there. Your team has to keep conducting audits in your business and ensure that every department is staying compliant. If there are potential gaps spotted, or key areas for improvement, you must take action immediately.

Seek legal advice and stay up-to-date

On top of all the points covered above, you should consult with a legal professional who is an expert with the laws and regulations involved in your industry. They can be there to guide you and ensure you implement effective compliance strategies while providing you with updated industry news and other valuable insights. The key here is to stay updated and always look beyond your company to understand what factors can affect your business in the near or distant future.

Protecting Your Intellectual Property Rights

Another important thing that I want to cover in this chapter is related to your intellectual property rights. This is often overlooked by entrepreneurs, and I am on a mission to address the overlooked bits in this book. Here is a simple step-by-step process that I implemented for my business:

- **Step 1: Identify your intellectual property assets**. The first step is to identify the different intellectual property assets you have in your LLC inventory. The various types include: trademarks, such as your company logo; domain name for branding purposes; copyrights, including any creative works that require protection; patents, such as inventions that only your company has made; and trade secrets, which are confidential information about the company's business operations and other processes.

- **Step 2: Understand the process of registering and protecting your IP**. The next step is to understand the various IP assets and what they require in terms of registration. For example, for registering your trademarks, like a brand name, logo, etc., you can check with your government agency. Whereas for patents, you will undergo a more complex and sophisticated registration process, since this is about protecting inventions. Furthermore, copyright protection is essential when it comes to protecting original creations, and your business will probably require a few of them to create a unique brand and reach out to clients.

- **Step 3: Implement strategies to protect trade secrets**. For protecting trade secrets, such as inside knowledge of your company and how your internal business runs (or any sensitive information), you can draft non-disclosure agreements (NDAs) and implement a management system so that employees are trained to not disclose any confidential information to any third party.

- **Step 4: Claim IP rights against infringement**. Having intellectual property rights in the first place is a defense mechanism to fight against potential infringement. If there is a situation where violations occur, such as third-party companies stealing your original creative work or employees disclosing confidential information to external parties, these rights help you to pursue legal action against the violators and also negotiate for compensation.

- **Step 5: Utilize contracts and stay updated with regulatory changes**. It is essential to have contacts and agreements in place to protect your IP assets. Ensure that you conduct regular auditing to review your IP rights protections under your LLC and also reach out for legal assistance to facilitate the process. Keep an eye on the market at all times and understand how IP rights can vary from region to region and from country to country (this will be essential if you plan to scale globally in the future).

Data Privacy and Implementing Cybersecurity Measures

In the final portion of this chapter, we will cover data privacy and cybersecurity. Protecting your data is another important pillar for building and protecting your business.

It is a legal requirement that businesses ensure data privacy and implement cybersecurity practices. You can study more about these with respect to relevant regulatory compliance by looking at the GDPR (General Data Protection Regulation), CCPA (Central Consumer Protection Authority), or any other related cybersecurity regulations.

Understanding the importance of data privacy and protection

Protecting your LLC against data breaches, hacking, or any related cybercrime is the responsibility of the entrepreneur and their management. This is a serious subject these days, as millions of financial transactions and pieces of data are being transferred digitally each day. Moreover, data privacy is an important aspect when it comes to protecting the information of your clients, suppliers, partners, and employees. Therefore, prioritizing the protection of sensitive data is an ethical necessity for any business.

Implementing data privacy procedures and policies

It is mandatory that you implement data privacy policies and procedures to outline how your company will handle confidential and sensitive information. For example, you should introduce strategies to protect the privacy of data collected from employees, clients, and partners. Then, implement procedures for the safe storage of data so you are less prone to data breaches. Furthermore, implement a system for authorized access control and data retrieval for business purposes and not for external reasons, such as third-party sharing.

Training employees on various cybersecurity practices

I believe everything starts internally in a business. The culture is important, and this is why I urge business owners to support a culture where employees and management are trained and educated on the importance of cybersecurity and data privacy. This helps you to utilize smart minds and come up with innovative solutions to protect data and mitigate risks of cyber crimes. For example, train your staff on the basic practices that can make a big impact in the grand scheme of things, such as how to use robust passwords and update them frequently, or how to transfer and access sensitive data safely without exposing it to public networks or other platforms.

Conducting regular security assessments and updating protocols

It is mandatory that you regularly conduct assessments and audits to find any flaws or room for improvement to ensure safe data-sharing practices and to mitigate cyber crimes. This is where your compliance department can play a huge role by coordinating with your IT officer and implementing safe practices in your organization. Update these protocols regularly based on legal regulations.

This chapter has provided you with a general overview of the importance of compliance management and staying updated with regulatory requirements. Staying prepared and mitigating risks along the way is crucial for any business, not just LLCs.

You can implement safe practices, such as having a compliance management system in place to constantly monitor and ensure that every department complies with the necessary regulations.

You can protect your IP assets, such as trademarks, copyrights, trade secrets, patents, etc. Implement safe data privacy and sharing practices, as well as other relevant cybersecurity practices.

Moreover, you can always use your insurance coverage, which we discussed in-depth in the previous chapters. This includes your general liability coverage and professional liability coverage, to name a few.

Key Takeaways From This Chapter

- It is important to identify business risks both internally and externally. Assess each risk's potential probability and consequences and develop risk mitigation strategies to minimize each threat.
- Ensure compliance with laws and regulations for your business by staying updated on industry-

specific laws and standards. Create rules and processes to comply with these legal requirements, and continually audit and evaluate your compliance management systems.

- Protect your intellectual property assets, such as trademarks, patents, copyrights, and trade secrets, by understanding the importance of safeguarding them and adopting registration processes to defend against potential infringement.

- Implement data privacy and cybersecurity measures in your LLC by understanding relevant cyber-related regulations, implementing ideal cybersecurity practices, training employees and management to comply with these standards, and constantly updating your protocols.

Chapter 11

Exiting Your LLC

Always have a backup plan to the backup plan.

— Gillian Flynn

I n this chapter, we will cover your options for exiting an LLC. You may be wondering why I've included a chapter on this topic. Even though this book is about motivating you to run a successful LLC, part of this career path is knowing how to exit when it's time to wind things down.

Many business owners are so optimistic that they overlook the possibility of failure and struggle to either sell or exit the business. However, this book covers it all, and I want to share some options for exiting your LLC. This chapter will cover exit options in-depth, including dissolving, selling the business, transferring ownership, and succession planning.

Having an exit strategy is necessary, and it should be stated in your operating agreement when you draft it. Once you've finished reading this chapter, write down your ideal exit strategy for your LLC and be sure it is included in your operating agreement.

Assessing Different Exiting Options for LLC Owners

It is worth noting that LLC owners have many exiting strategies they can consider when they are ready to move away from the LLC model. These strategies include the following:

Dissolution: The act of liquidating assets in an LLC in order to wind down or close.

Selling: The act of transferring ownership of your LLC in exchange for monetary compensation. For example, Owner A sells their LLC to New Owner B.

Transfer ownership: Not exactly selling but transferring ownership to your close family members, business partners, or even, in some cases, employees.

Initial Public Offering: The act of taking your company public by issuing shares on the regulatory stock exchange (as we learned about with the corporation model).

Merger: The act of combining the LLC with another company while combining both companies' assets and liabilities.

Acquisition: The act of your LLC being acquired or purchased by a larger business entity.

As you can see, there are many options to choose from. However, in this chapter, we will cover mainly dissolution, selling, and transferring ownership.

Assessing financial and legal implications

Though there are several exiting options available to you, it is vital that you understand that each option does have various financial and legal implications behind it. For instance, dissolving your LLC means you receive net asset sales, but you will need to take care of other factors, such as settling your debts or liabilities. You will also need to account for tax-related considerations.

This can apply to the option of selling your LLC as well. But the friction involved in selling has to do with the negotiations and finding the right valuation and price for your LLC sale.

Transferring ownership to either a family member or business partner will involve a lot of legal contracts and agreements. Moreover, this option requires future tax planning and ensuring that the stage is set for a smooth transfer of ownership.

Various complications will pop up with other exit strategies as well, such as IPO. For an initial public offering, your business needs to meet specific regulatory requirements with respect to the stock exchange and also implement practices such as public reporting and facing public scrutiny.

Assessing personal and business goals

When you start considering and planning to exit your LLC, you'll need to think about your personal and business goals first and foremost. It is natural for entrepreneurs to be susceptible to emotional factors in making an exiting decision, but you will need to look at the grand scheme of things and how it will affect your professional and personal life, not to mention those around you who are involved, such as your family members, employees, and other stakeholders.

Ask yourself why you want to do it. Do you want to pursue an exiting strategy in order to optimize your business's profits? Do you want your company's legacy to stay safe in someone else's hands? What long-term consequences might exiting your LLC hold for both your personal life and career? It is crucial to take your time and assess all options; you might find that exiting at your current stage is not the best idea after all.

Seeking professional advice to evaluate the best course of action

For situations like these, it is recommended that you reach out to professionals who can help you through the process and advise you regarding next steps. For example, you can reach out to professionals such as financial and legal advisors to help you assess the financial and legal implications of exiting, as well as the effect it can have on your business or personal financial goals. They will also clarify your tax consequences and legal agreements, as well as how to align with regulatory requirements.

You can also reach out to business valuators to assess and determine the valuation of your LLC should you decide to sell to a third party. These professionals can help you get a good price for the empire you have built while also facilitating the smooth transfer of business ownership.

Understanding the Process of Dissolving an LLC

Let's take a closer look at the process of dissolving an LLC. As you already know, dissolution is the act of liquidating the LLC's assets and winding down the business. Despite how simple the definition sounds, there are many things you will need to account for and consider during this process.

Understanding the process and legal requirements for LLC dissolution

The first thing you need to understand is what LLC dissolution actually means legally. It basically refers to the complete termination of the existence of your business entity. There are various legal requirements for dissolution depending on the state your business is registered in. If you are based in the U.S. specifically, each state can have varying procedures that you need to adhere to.

Notifying stakeholders and creditors about the potential dissolution

In the event of dissolving your LLC, it is your obligation to notify your stakeholders in advance of this big move. These will include your business partners, shareholder members, management, employees, clients, suppliers, and also your creditors. Clearly communicate the intent behind dissolving your LLC and also provide a timeline for when it will happen.

Settling outstanding debts and obligations of the LLC

The next important step in the process is to ensure that all outstanding debts, liabilities, and other obligations of the LLC are settled. This should happen before finalizing the dissolution of your LLC. Settling outstanding debts and obligations might include paying off your existing creditors and suppliers or settling other financial obligations which have been left pending.

Distributing assets among members

Once the obligations and debts have been settled, it is crucial to distribute the assets among members with respect to what was agreed upon and outlined in the operating agreement. "What if I didn't mention asset distribution in my operating agreement?" you might ask. "What happens then?" Then by default, the state where you registered your LLC will determine the asset distribution allocation.

Complying with state laws and filing paperwork for dissolution

Speaking of state law, this is another important step in the dissolution process. You have to comply with specific state laws by filing the necessary paperwork. You will need to fulfill final tax obligations at the local, state, and federal level and cancel any related business licenses, permits, registrations, etc. You will then cancel any other contracts, such as leases, agreements, and other related subscriptions.

The final actions of dissolving an LLC include submitting a formal dissolution document to the agency in your state, and then notifying of the intent to dissolve the LLC. An extra tip I would recommend here is to retain important records and documents related to your LLC for future tax purposes or legal inquiries.

Understanding the Process of Selling an LLC

Let us now switch gears to the process of selling your LLC. Selling an LLC is basically transferring ownership of the business to another party. Let us go through the steps and factors you will need to account for to successfully sell your LLC.

Conducting a business valuation to determine your LLC's worth

The entire process of selling an LLC starts with understanding how much your LLC is worth. For this, you will need to conduct a business valuation. You can go about this by assessing several factors, such as your business's financial performance throughout the years, your number of assets versus liabilities, and also the various market trends and industry potential, to determine whether your business is worth more or less in a particular market or industry.

Preparing your LLC for the sale

Selling your LLC doesn't mean you should rush and just simply hand it off to someone else. It should be done in an organized manner, and this means utilizing essential documents, such as your contracts, leases, agreements, financial records, tax returns, and so on. All these documents should be safely retrievable and organized so that you can show them to the potential buyer. Moreover, you should communicate openly in advance to your employees and management about the potential sale, as this action could mean a complete overhaul of their work lives and careers.

Identifying potential buyers and negotiating the terms of the sale

Buyers won't come to you automatically. It is your job to identify potential buyers who can meet your business's long-term vision and value to sustain your legacy. Use your business connections and word-of-mouth to help you find the right fit. When it comes to negotiating the terms of the sale, you will need to specify the basics, including the purchasing price, the payment structure, and any other clauses to be included. Moreover, you might consider including a non-disclosure agreement when negotiating with potential buyers in order to protect sensitive business information, such as trade secrets, because not all potential buyers you meet are going to end up following through on the deal after seeing this information.

Drafting a purchase agreement and completing the sale

After verbally agreeing to the terms with the buyer, your next step is to draft a legally binding purchase agreement. This document will typically outline the details, such as price for the sale, assets being transferred over, and certain clauses such as warranties, indemnification, etc. After completing the sale transaction, there will be a transfer of funds and owner-ship assets as specified in the purchase agreement.

Seeking legal and financial guidance to facilitate the process

In a nutshell, selling an LLC isn't the same as selling a product or service in your business. It is a complex procedure. Hence, it will be important to consult with professionals, such as financial advisors and your business attorneys who specialize in this area. With a lot at stake involving financial, legal, operational, and tax considerations, as well as documentation and negotiating terms, having professionals at your side will be invaluable.

Transferring Ownership and Succession Planning

So what all is entailed in the process of transferring ownership and succession planning? Transferring ownership in this case is the act of passing down your business ownership to close contacts, such as family members, partners, or employees. It differs from a sale because it doesn't involve an exchange of funds for transferring ownership, but it will be important to familiarize yourself with this particular process.

Early planning for transfer of ownership

If it is your intention to transfer ownership to existing members or new partners, it is vital to plan for a smooth execution. You will be considering factors such as who will take over the business and their intent. You need to ask yourself what makes this person or group of members worthy of ownership, and whether your legacy will be carried through to the future. You also need to account for the timing of when this potential ownership transfer will occur and ensure it doesn't come at a bad time, like in the course of the financial year, for instance.

Identifying and grooming potential successors

When you are identifying possible successors within your LLC, it is important to make sure that they will be ready to actually succeed you. This can be done by providing them with mentorship and sufficient entrepreneurial training, and also making clear the role and responsibilities they will be taking on when this move happens. Good communication early on will help you vet your potential successor and discover whether they are the right fit to take over. It is better to take it slow and be sure rather than rushing and handing over the business to them only to regret it later when your business is failing.

Drafting a comprehensive succession plan for the transition

The next step involves drafting a succession plan that outlines the entire transitioning process. This includes outlining a summary of the ownership transfer, the updated roles of the leaders, their responsibilities, the new decision-making and communication structure, and also the timeline for this transfer to occur. If there are any potential risks involved in the transfer, this is where you will include emergency backup plans.

Ensuring a smooth transfer of responsibilities and management control

For an ownership transfer to be considered successful, you will need to ensure that everything goes smoothly—mainly the transfer of responsibilities and management control. Therefore, as I specified earlier, having transparent and open communication about the situation and outlining the entire process in documented form will help to make the process easier and prevent potential regrets.

Addressing tax and legal considerations in ownership transfers and succession planning

As a final tip and precaution, ensure that any tax or legal requirements are fulfilled with regard to the ownership transfer or succession planning. Some common financial implications that may arise in an ownership transfer include estate taxes and capital gains taxes. Therefore, you need to ensure that your LLC's operating agreement complies with the relevant state laws for a seamless transfer of ownership.

Winding Down and Finalizing LLC Affairs

We will conclude this chapter by briefly going through the process of winding down and finalizing all the affairs related to your LLC.

This will act as a summary for the steps you need to take before officially closing or exiting your LLC. Follow this checklist and keep it close for quick reference as you check off each step.

The following things need to be addressed:

- Settle any pending financial obligations and close accounts.
- Notify government agencies, clients, partners, and vendors about the LLC closure.
- Dispose of assets, close offices, and cancel business licenses, permits, and registrations (if necessary).
- Retain essential and important records and documents for legal purposes.
- File final tax returns and fulfill the necessary tax obligations.
- Seek legal advice and guidance to ensure legal compliance in the winding down process (optional).

When you follow these steps diligently, you will be able to wind down your LLC legally and also finalize any affairs in the process. This is how you exit an LLC in an organized and compliant manner. In the final chapter, we will look at next steps that go beyond the topic of an LLC.

Key Takeaways From This Chapter

- LLC owners have several exiting options available to them. These include dissolution, selling, transferring ownership, succession planning, merger, acquisition, and initial public offering.
- Dissolving an LLC is liquidating the business's assets for closure. It involves notifying the stakeholders and creditors about the intent to dissolve, settling outstanding obligations, distributing assets among members according to the operating agreement, and complying with state laws regarding the necessary paperwork and filing.
- Selling an LLC is transferring ownership of the business in exchange for monetary compensation. It involves determining the business's worth, identifying potential buyers, negotiating the terms of the sale, drafting a purchase agreement, and completing the sale.
- Transferring ownership involves passing down the business to close contacts, such as family members, partners, or employees. It involves a lot of succession planning, identifying the right successor, and grooming them for success. You will also need to address tax and legal considerations and outline an effective succession plan for a smooth transition process.

Chapter 12

Growing Beyond the LLC—Next Steps

Develop a passion for learning. If you do, you will never cease to grow.

— Anthony J. D'Angelo

We are approaching the end of this book, and you have learned a lot about forming and running an LLC. This final chapter will be a short one, and I will provide you with some brief insights on how to grow beyond the LLC.

We will walk through transitioning your LLC to another business entity, planning for long-term business growth, and the importance of seeking professional advice and support throughout your tenure as an entrepreneur.

Transitioning to a Different Business Entity

Transitioning your LLC to a different business entity can require a lot of thinking on your part. For instance, you have to ensure that your decision to transition to a different entity aligns with your long-term business goals, and the intent should be justified. Moreover, communicating the transition to all stakeholders and knowing how it can influence your day-to-day operations should be right up there on your priority list.

Exploring other business entities and evaluating the benefits and drawbacks

You might consider various options as alternatives to your LLC. The common ones include those that we learned about in earlier chapters, and they include corporations (specifically S corporations), partnerships, and sole proprietorships. Let us assess each option in brief so that you may recall their pros and cons:

- **Sole proprietorship**: If you transition into this business entity, you are welcoming simplicity when it comes to running operations, record-keeping, and tax filing. However, it completely removes the limited liability protection you had with an LLC.
- **Partnership**: If you transition into this business entity, you will have better flexibility with tax treatment but will have to deal with shared liability among partners. For example, you could be held liable for your partner's actions.
- **Corporation**: If you transition into this business entity, you will have better scope of raising funding for your business—especially through issuing stocks —but it requires going through complex procedures, and there are many regulatory requirements as well.
- **S Corp**: This particular corporation structure will guarantee that you keep the pass-through taxation

benefit you had with your LLC and also your limited liability protection. However, that's *if* you qualify for it, because it requires meeting certain eligibility criteria.

Understanding legal and financial implications

What you can understand from the above options is that no matter what you decide to transition to, there will be a few implications involved—especially legal and financial ones. Transitioning requires a lot of legal procedures, so seeking professional guidance from legal advisors and attorneys can help you understand the entire legal process and the implications behind transitioning, such as filing the right documents and meeting certain regulatory requirements. Moreover, you will need to understand how it will affect your tax filings and whether there will be necessary changes to your tax forms you need to file, the deadlines, the tax rates, and other tax-related obligations.

Planning for Long-term Business Growth and Sustainability

In this section, we will go through a brief step-by-step method for planning long-term business growth and also ensuring sustainability for decades.

Setting strategic goals and objectives for the future

The first step involves goal planning. You will need to define clear, measurable goals that will provide you with a clear vision toward which you can direct your business. Most entrepreneurs should have a 10-year vision plan, for starters, to understand where they want their business to be in 10 years or so.

Developing a growth roadmap and action plan

The next step is to create a roadmap for encouraging growth and actions to achieve your goals. In my opinion, the best way to do this is by setting milestones. For example, for your 10-year target, break it down into milestones of 3-year plans. Then, break those down into 1-year plans. Doing this will make it easier for you to understand the tasks and important goals in line to achieve that 10-year-plus target. You can then develop strategic action plans to achieve the smaller objectives set for each year.

Identifying opportunities for diversification or expansion into new markets

The third fundamental step in any entrepreneur's mind should be to train themselves to identify opportunities. This might include diversifying your products and service offerings in order to make them more unique, or building a sustainable revenue stream. Or, you might expand into new markets that will encourage growth for your business or brand.

Building a scalable infrastructure

The next step you should take—and it is an important step in building a sustainable organization—is to focus on infrastructure. If you can build a strong infrastructure that enables your team to strive for incremental growth, then this will lead your business to great things. For instance, the areas involved in building a scalable infrastructure include bringing in top talent and retaining the best people as part of your plans, streamlining and optimizing your work processes to keep delivering results and efficiency, and lastly, investing in updated technology and software solutions that will take your operations to the next level.

Continuously monitoring and adapting to evolving market conditions

The last step in this long-term cycle involves constantly monitoring the performance of your organization using key metrics or KPIs to ensure you are aligned with your growth objectives. In addition, it is essential to adapt your business strategy to evolving changes in the market or industry so that you can survive and come out on top against your competitors in the long run.

Seeking Professional Advice and Support

I will conclude this chapter by going through one final thing, and this is an important factor to consider as an entrepreneur, no matter what kind of business you are running. *Make the best of the people around you.* This was the sole reason why I was able to succeed in my own business. It was not because I was technically gifted or the "Albert Einstein" of all entrepreneurs; it was because of the people in my life and my strong network. To conclude this book, I will leave you with four important lessons that you should digest as you get ready to run your own LLC or any other business venture.

- **Recognize the value of professional expertise in running and growing a business**. Ensure that you understand the value and important role of your professionals in the success of your business. You must keep bringing in talent that have professional expertise so they can bring in more experience and insights to solve complex business challenges and make the right decisions without the need for supervision.

- **Engage with attorneys, accountants, and business consultants for guidance**. Always keep your attorneys and accountants close. Attorneys are the experts who are there for legal guidance, and your accountants are there to keep your business financially sound. In addition, I recommend seeking external guidance, such as business consultants, if you are facing a rut in your business and need expert help.

- **Build a network of mentors and industry professionals for support**. Relationships, relationships, relationships. Having a network of experts who can keep providing value over time is a must. So, prioritize your relationships with suppliers, mentors, and other industry professionals so that you keep bringing in value to your business.

- **Continue learning and stay updated on industry trends and best practices**. As an entrepreneur, you are continuously learning; even if you've achieved all the business objectives out there, you aren't done yet. Keep seeking guidance and learn more by attending webinars, workshops, or industry conferences. There are always new things to learn about in your industry, so expand your creative base to revolutionize your business. Embrace a lifelong learning mindset so that you can foster your personal and professional growth.

Key Takeaways From This Chapter

- Transitioning your LLC into a different business entity can be a process that requires a lot of careful thinking. The options available to you include sole proprietorship, partnership, corporation, or S corporation.
- It is crucial to set a long-term vision growth plan for your business by setting growth objectives, developing a growth roadmap and action plan, identifying opportunities for diversification and expansion, building a scalable infrastructure, and continuously monitoring and adapting to the evolving market.
- The four vital lessons when it comes to seeking ongoing professional advice and support are: recognize professional expertise to grow your business; engage with attorneys, accountants, and business consultants for guidance; build a network of mentors and industry professionals that provide value; and continue learning and embracing a growth mindset.

Conclusion

Desire is the starting point of all achievement, not a hope, not a wish, but a keen pulsating desire which transcends everything.

— Napoleon Hill

I thank you for completing this book, and I hope you have acquired tons of knowledge that will help you to form and run a successful LLC business. In this book, you have learned the following:

- the basic legal structure of an LLC
- comparisons with other business structures and how you can choose the right structure for your LLC
- steps to form your LLC
- how to manage and operate your LLC business
- the importance of liability protection as an LLC owner
- the taxation guide for your LLC
- how you can keep financing your LLC

- the different contracts and legal agreements associated with an LLC
- steps to scale and grow your LLC
- how to conduct risk management and the compliance side of things
- strategies to exit your LLC
- the next steps to grow beyond your LLC

If you enjoyed the knowledge you received from this book, I urge you to share your honest review with other aspiring entrepreneurs who are looking to dive deep and learn more about pursuing an LLC or entrepreneurship in general.

>> Leave a review on Amazon US <<
>> Leave a review on Amazon UK <<

References

5 Common Types Of Business Contracts You May Need | Henke & Williams LLP. (2022, February 8). https://www.henkelawfirm.com/blog/litigation/business/5-common-types-of-business-contracts-you-may-need/

10 Types of Business Loans: Compare Financing. (n.d.). NerdWallet. https://www.nerdwallet.com/article/small-business/types-of-business-loans

A Comprehensive Guide to LLC Taxes - SmartAsset. (n.d.). Smartasset.com. https://smartasset.com/taxes/how-llcs-are-taxed

Altaf, Y. (2023, February 8). *7 Crucial Ways To Scale Your Startup or Business*. Entrepreneur. https://www.entrepreneur.com/growing-a-business/7-crucial-ways-to-scale-your-startup-or-business/443794

Ansarada. (n.d.). *Your Business Exit Strategy - 8 Types of Exit Strategies*. Ansarada. https://www.ansarada.com/business-exits/strategies

Apply for licenses and permits. (2020). Apply for Licenses and Permits. https://www.sba.gov/business-guide/launch-your-business/apply-licenses-permits

Corporate Veil Theory. (n.d.). VEDANTU. https://www.vedantu.com/commerce/corporate-veil-theory

Esq, P. L. (2022, February 28). *Does an LLC Always Protect Against Personal Liability?* Law Offices of Peter J. Lamont. https://www.pjlesq.com/post/does-an-llc-always-protect-against-personal-liability

Fitzpatrick, D., & J.D. (n.d.). *Funding Your LLC*. Nolo. https://www.nolo.com/legal-encyclopedia/funding-your-llc.html

Funding Your Company: Top 9 Ways to Finance Your LLC or Corporation. (n.d.). MyCompanyWorks. https://www.mycompanyworks.com/funding-your-company-top-ways-to-finance-your-llc-or-corporation/

Get a Certificate of Organization or Formation for Your New LLC. (n.d.). The Balance. https://www.thebalancemoney.com/certificate-of-organization-398183#

Haskins, J. (2019, May 29). *How to Start an LLC in 7 Steps*. Legalzoom. https://www.legalzoom.com/articles/how-to-start-an-llc-in-7-steps

How to Operate an LLC: Everything You Need to Know. (n.d.). UpCounsel. https://www.upcounsel.com/how-to-operate-an-llc

How to Plan for Exiting an LLC. (2018, September 25). IncNow. https://www.incnow.com/blog/2018/09/25/llc-member-exit-strategy/

LLC Members vs. LLC Managers - How They Differ | BizFilings. (n.d.).

References

Www.wolterskluwer.com. https://www.wolterskluwer.com/en/expert-insights/llc-members-vs-llc-managerswho-are-they-and-how-are-they-different

LLC Operating Agreement Requirements by State. (n.d.). Www.rocket-lawyer.com. https://www.rocketlawyer.com/business-and-contracts/start ing-a-business/form-an-llc/legal-guide/llc-operating-agreement-requirements-by-state

Robinson, G. (2022, March 11). *How To Keep Your LLC Compliant.* The Robinson Advocacy Group. https://www.therobinsonadvocacygroup.com/how-to-keep-your-llc-compliant

Section 179: Definition, How It Works, and Example. (n.d.). Investopedia. https://www.investopedia.com/terms/s/section-179.asp#

Simon, D. (n.d.). *The Different Types of LLCs.* Tailor Brands. https://www.tailorbrands.com/llc-formation/types-of-llc

Starting a business: A license and permit checklist. (n.d.). Legalzoom. https://www.legalzoom.com/articles/starting-a-business-a-license-and-permit-checklist

Stowers, J. (2022, August 4). *How to Choose the Best Legal Structure for Your Business.* Business News Daily. https://www.businessnewsdaily.com/8163-choose-legal-business-structure.html

Tax credit. (2023, August 18). Wikipedia. https://en.wikipedia.org/wiki/Tax_credit#

The 5 Largest U.S. Product Liability Cases. (2019). Investopedia. https://www.investopedia.com/the-5-largest-u-s-product-liability-cases-4773418

The Complete Guide to LLC Taxes. (n.d.). Bench. https://bench.co/blog/tax-tips/llc-taxes

The Small Business Owner and Product Liability. (n.d.). Findlaw. https://www.findlaw.com/smallbusiness/liability-and-insurance/the-small-busi ness-owner-and-product-liability.html

Watts, R. (2021, May 6). *How To Set Up An LLC In 7 Steps.* Forbes Advisor. https://www.forbes.com/advisor/business/how-to-set-up-an-llc-in-7-steps/

Who Is a Registered Agent & Do You Need One? (n.d.). StartGlobal. https://startglobal.co/registered-agent